Beverly Thomas Galloway

Commercial Violet Culture

A Treatise on the growing and marketing of Violets for Profit

Beverly Thomas Galloway

Commercial Violet Culture
A Treatise on the growing and marketing of Violets for Profit

ISBN/EAN: 9783337106508

Printed in Europe, USA, Canada, Australia, Japan

Cover: Foto ©ninafisch / pixelio.de

More available books at **www.hansebooks.com**

COMMERCIAL
VIOLET CULTURE.

A Treatise on the Growing and Marketing
of Violets for Profit.

BY

B. T. GALLOWAY,

Chief of the Division of Vegetable Physiology and Pathology,
United States Department of Agriculture.

NEW YORK.
A. T. DE LA MARE PTG. & PUB. CO. Ltd.
1899.

PREFACE.

Violet growing as a business has not received the attention given to some other crops. This is probably due to the fact that the violet as generally grown is less profitable than the rose, carnation, or even the chrysanthemum. More people have embarked in this business and failed than is the case with any other crop, and for this reason we believe that it is one of the most promising fields for the young, energetic, and intelligent man to enter. Whoever enters it, however, must recognize at the start that there are many difficulties, and that to be successful means much labor, patience, and determination to overcome all obstacles. The knowledge necessary to succeed can come only through experience. Reading will help, but without the ability to apply what is learned by reading little progress can be made. We have gone over this ground pretty thoroughly, and in looking back can see that our experience in many cases was dearly bought. To save others from making mistakes that fell to our lot we have in some instances made statements which might be considered as dogmatic. We have done this for the reason that we were many times led away by general statements, which, had they been specific would have saved us much time and money. We have endeavored to give every necessary detail for handling the soil, erection of houses and frames, the management of the plants, and marketing of the flowers, and finally we have shown what it costs to grow a violet plant, what such a plant under fair conditions should yield, and what in our experience may be looked upon as a fair profit.

From the facts given it will be seen that no big fortunes are to be made in violet growing, but if a man loves Nature and that quiet and peace which work with her should always bring, there is a chance here to open her doors. Thus a love for all that is good and beautiful may be cultivated and a respectable living made at the same time.

I wish to express my thanks to Mr. P. H. Dorsett, who shared with me all the trials and vexations which fall to the lot of beginners in this work. He is now a successful grower and many of the illustrations given are from his houses.

B. T. GALLOWAY.

WASHINGTON, D. C.,
      July 1st, 1899.

TABLE OF CONTENTS.

CHAPTER I.

Page

Introduction........................ 17
    Single Varieties................... 17
        Russian Violet................. 17
        Welsiana...................... 17
        Luxonne...................... 18
        California, or Madame E. Arene....... 18
        Princess of Wales, or Princesse de Galles... 18
    Double Varieties.................. 19
        Neapolitan.................... 19
        Lady Hume Campbell............. 19
        Marie Louise................... 19
        Farquhar and Imperial............. 20
    Origin and Introduction of Varieties........ 20
    Culture, Past and Present.............. 25

CHAPTER II.

The Soil........................... 30

CHAPTER III.

Construction of Houses and Frames.......... 43
    Construction of Houses............... 43
    Construction of Frames............... 77

CHAPTER IV.

Water Supply....................... 88

CHAPTER V.

Propagating, Selecting, Planting, Cleaning, Watering,
    etc. 92
    Propagating 92
    Selection of Stock for Vigor and Productiveness . . 109
    Planting 116
    Cleaning, Watering, Syringing, Mulching, and
        Feeding 124

CHAPTER VI.

Temperature Conditions and Ventilation 130

CHAPTER VII.

Handling and Marketing the Crop 140

CHAPTER VIII.

Diseases and Insect Enemies 159
    Diseases and their Treatment 159
        Spot, or Spot Disease 161
        Wilt, or Stem Rot 170
        Nanism, or Stuntedness 174
        Scald, or Edge Burn 178
        Oedema, or Wart Disease 182
        Crown Rot 185
        Root Galls, or Nematodes 187
    Insects and Other Pests 190
        Red Spider 190
        Green and Brown Aphides 198
        Cut Worms 208
        Sawfly 210
        Gall Fly Maggots 211
        Phlyctænia ferrugalis 214

CHAPTER IX.

Cost of Production and Profits 216

ILLUSTRATIONS.

		Page
FRONTISPIECE.		
1.	Type of Single Violet	21
2.	Type of Double Violet.	23
3.	Characteristic Growth of California and Marie Louise Compared	24
4.	Mixing Soil. Spreading Manure in Layers Between the Soil	36
5.	Mixing Soil. Breaking and Pulverizing the Sod Preparatory to Putting it down with Layers of Manure	37
6.	Sash House with Sash off.	44
7.	House twelve feet wide, six feet to Ridge; side ventilators of glass.	45
8.	Type of Even Span House, twelve feet wide, showing Method of Running Heating Pipes and Constructing Beds	46
9.	Type of Even Span House, twelve feet wide, with two deep walks, showing Heating Pipes and Method of Constructing Beds, Roofs, and Ends	48
10.	Shed at North End of Houses, showing Method of Construction	49
11.	Interior of Shed shown in fig. 10.	50
12.	Roofs of Twelve Foot Houses, showing Method of Construction and of Attaching Ventilators . .	51
13.	A Twelve Foot House, showing Method of Constructing and Attaching Side Ventilators . . .	54
14.	Fastening Pipes to Posts by Tin Clips	57
15.	Fastening Pipes to Posts by Bent Wire Nails . . .	5

		Page
16.	Interior of Twelve Foot House, showing Method of Constructing South End and Door	58
17.	Interior of House, showing Method of Connecting Flow Pipe with Four Returns	59
18.	Ridge and Furrow House Construction. Method of Making Gutter and Attaching Sash Bar	60
19.	Interior Construction. Method of Connecting Returns at North End of House	61
20.	Construction of Single House. Method of Making Gutter, Attaching Sash Bar, and Fitting Side Ventilators	62
21.	Method of Splicing Ridge	64
22.	House twenty-four feet wide	65
23.	Constructing House twenty-four feet wide; Second Step, Making Beds and Walks	66
24.	Constructing House twenty-four feet wide; Third Step, Running Gutters and Notching Plate around Posts	67
25.	Construction. Putting Up the Roof	72
26.	Temporary House	76
27.	Simple Cold Frame	78
28.	Violets in Frame, Covered with Lath Screen	80
29.	Violets in Heated Frames, Shaded by Rough Boards	82
30.	Violets in Heated Frames. Summer Shading by Boards	84
31.	Cuttings with Hard, Wiry Roots, from Divided Crowns	93
32.	Various Kinds of Cuttings from a Divided Crown	94
33.	Common Form of Cutting from Divided Crown	96
34.	Lath Box, or Flat, for Rooted Cuttings	98
35.	Sand-Rooted Cuttings, Ready to Plant in Flats Filled with Soil	102
36.	Sand-Rooted Cuttings, Ideal Type, Ready to Put in Soil	104

		Page
37.	Pedigree Plant, with Tag showing Dates of Picking and Yield of Flowers	110
38.	Bed of Pedigree Plants	112
39.	Violet Culture Under Lath Sheds in California	120
40.	Field Culture of Violets in Virginia	122
41.	Violets bunched for Philadelphia market; some of the flowers projecting from the bunch	142
42.	Violets bunched for Washington market, using Princess of Wales leaves	144
43.	Picking Violets	150
44.	Leaves of California Violet Wired Together for Bunching Flowers	152
45.	Leatherette Shipping Box, Open	154
46.	Shipping Box, showing Wire Screen for Holding Bunches	155
47.	Shipping Box, Closed and Strapped	156
48.	Spot Disease—Early Effects	162
49.	Spot Disease on Hardy English Violets	164
50.	Spot Disease Artificially Produced	166
51.	Rooted Campbell Cuttings, showing Effects of Thielavia on the roots	171
52.	Plants Stunted by Strong Fertilizer	175
53.	Edge Burn, brought on by Cold Soil	178
54.	Leaves and Flowers Injured by Botrytis	180
55.	Oedema, or Wart Disease	183
56.	Crown Rot	185
57.	Nematodes, or Root Galls	188
58.	Nozzle Used in Spraying Plants for the Destruction of Red Spider	192
59.	Method of Determining Cubic Contents of Houses	204
60.	Injuries to Violet Leaves by Gall Fly Maggot	212
61.	Larvæ and Moths of *Phlyctænia ferrugalis*	214

COMMERCIAL VIOLET CULTURE.

CHAPTER I.

INTRODUCTION.

The sweet violet, Viola odorata, from which our cultivated forms have doubtless arisen, is widely distributed over Europe and Asia, but is not found native in America. The violet has been cultivated from remote times, first probably as a medicinal plant, but later to satisfy a love for the beautiful. Following are some of the more important forms now grown:

SINGLE VARIETIES.

Russian Violet. Very hardy and free flowering; flowers medium violet* in color, fairly good size.

Welsiana. Plant much branched; foliage

---

*In referring to the colors of violets we have used Ridgway's Nomenclature of Colors, published by Little, Brown & Co., Boston. The principal colors are the true violet, as will be found in Princess of Wales, and the various shades of mauve. Mauves are a mixture of white with violet. The mauves therefore may be dark or light, depending upon the amount of white present. Marie Louise is a true mauve; Campbell a light mauve.

rather soft, light green; flowers large, on long stalks; color true violet; a valuable variety, but not so amenable to culture as some others.

Luxonne. A valuable variety, with large flowers of a dark violet color; foliage stronger in texture and of a richer green than the ordinary Russian violet; flowers from September to spring.

California, or Madame E. Arené. We use the name California because it has become so well established that it is not practicable at this time to change it. This violet is unquestionably one of the most valuable of the single sorts. The plant grows like a weed and flowers pretty regularly throughout the entire winter; foliage soft and lightish green in color; flowers large, light violet in color, with stems sometimes eight inches to a foot in length.

Princess of Wales, or Princesse de Galles. All things considered, this is the best single violet that has come to our attention. The plant is very vigorous and has the compact habit of growth of the double sorts; leaves dark rich green, of firm texture, making them very valuable for bunching; flowers large, of a true rich violet color, and borne on long, strong stems.

There are single violets white, yellow, and pink in color, but it is not necessary to give any details in regard to them, for the reason that there is practically no commercial demand for them.

DOUBLE VARIETIES.

Neapolitan. One of the oldest of the double sorts and doubtless the parent of a number of our most valuable varieties; growth compact; leaves rather small; flowers pushing up straight through the crown, borne on strong, straight stems; color very light mauve (commonly called light lavender); hardy and comparatively free flowering; blooms from September to spring.

Lady Hume Campbell. More vigorous than the last, with larger leaves and flowers; the flowers push up through the crown and stand above the leaves on straight, strong stems; color of the flowers, when properly grown, a mauve, several shades lighter than Marie Louise; flowers freely and continuously from September to May and is comparatively free from disease.

Marie Louise. The most widely cultivated violet in this country, and the one for which there is the greatest demand. This violet is not so vigorous as the last and is therefore more subject to the attacks of a number of diseases; the leaves are large, of a rich green color, but inclined to be soft; the flowers push out from the sides of the crown and are usually found resting on the ground; flower stalks not so straight as Campbell, making the flowers more difficult to bunch; color of flowers true mauve; base of petals white, splotched with red. The red marks are very characteristic of this variety and never occur, so far as we are aware, in any except closely related strains.

Farquhar and Imperial. Both of these forms, so far as we have been able to determine, are merely vigorous strains of Marie Louise.

Of other double varieties there may be mentioned Swanley White (pure white) and Madam Millet (pink). Both of these are occasionally grown, but there is no great demand for them anywhere.

ORIGIN AND INTRODUCTION OF VARIETIES.

Single violets in this country are as yet in comparatively little demand, and for this reason Marie Louise and Campbell are the principal varieties grown. There seems to be a growing interest in singles, however, and on this account and furthermore for the reason that the leaves are exceedingly useful in bunching, it would be well for every grower to devote a part of his space to some vigorous-growing kind like California or Princess of Wales. Six or seven hundred plants of either of these varieties will, with good cultivation, give sufficient leaves for bunching the flowers from eight thousand Campbell or Louise. In this way the foliage of the Campbell and Louise is left to support the flowers—a great advantage in many ways. The California and Princess of Wales, furthermore, will yield a sufficient number of flowers to well pay for the space devoted to them, so that altogether it is an advantage to have them.

ORIGIN AND INTRODUCTION OF VARIETIES. 21

1.—*Type of single violet (Princess of Wales), reduced one-third.*

There has been much discussion as to the origin of the Marie Louise and Campbell violets. The Marie Louise has been known under various names in France and Germany for sixty or seventy years. It was introduced into this country in 1871 by Mr. John Cook, of Baltimore. Mr. Cook obtained the stock through Schuer, of Heidelberg, Germany, who advertised it as the best violet belonging to the Parma class. After growing it for two years Mr. Cook sold large quantities of his stock to Peter Henderson and John Henderson, of New York, and Mr. Dreer, of Philadelphia. The flowers created a sensation and the plants in consequence were in great demand.

We find a record of the Lady Hume Campbell violet as far back as 1884 in the Gardeners' Chronicle, of London, England. It is said here that the variety had been seen growing in the gardens of Harefield Court, Rickmansworth, and that it was exceedingly vigorous. It was regarded as a vigorous strain of Neapolitan. It is stated further that the variety had been brought from abroad several years before by Lady Hume Campbell, and planted in her gardens at Highgrove, Waltford. Soon after it was noticed at Lady Campbell's place by a Mr. Turner, who bought the stock and presumably put it on the market. It was imported in 1892 by Mr. H. Heubner, of Groton, Massachusetts, who obtained

2.—*Type of double violet (Marie Louise), reduced one-third.*

his stock from Beachy, in Devonshire, England. Mr. Heubner informs the writer that he imported the so-called "De Parme" at the same time and he considers it to be in every way identical with Campbell. Parme de Toulouse

3.—*Characteristic growth of California (single) and Marie Louise (double) compared.*

and Parme sans Filet, both grown for a number of years in France and catalogued by Millet and others, seem to be the same as Campbell. It is probable, therefore, that the Campbell originated on the continent of Europe, that it was brought to England about 1879 or 1880, and was imported into the United States in 1892 or possibly earlier. Be that as it may, the variety has made a place for itself, and is now, owing to its great vigor and productiveness, gradually taking the place of the Marie Louise.

CULTURE PAST AND PRESENT.

Of the early days of violet growing in this country, that is, the work as it was carried on up to fifteen years ago, little need be said. In most cases the methods employed were crude when looked at from the present point of view, just as our methods will, no doubt, be considered crude by those who follow us. The plants for the most part were grown in frames or in pots, under the mistaken idea that it was necessary to have them near the glass. Even now, despite the rapid advances made in greenhouse construction, it is rare to find a modern violet establishment in the true sense of the word. Sash houses are still largely in vogue, and little resembling the compact, business-like structures used for carnations and roses are to be found. We have often been at a loss to account for this, except on the ground that the plant is really one which at times will do fairly well under seemingly very poor treatment, while again all the coaxing and luxurious surroundings imaginable cannot make it thrive. It is a truth well established that more people go into violet growing and fail than is the case with the growing of any other crop under glass. Time and time again we have seen men start into the business with no experience and nothing but the poorest kind of equipment and succeed for the first two or three years in a truly remarkable way. Then trouble comes in one form or another and in two or three years more the grower has passed out of the field. It requires about five years to definitely determine what a man with ordinary facilities can do in this matter. Of course he will have his ups and downs and the temptation will be strong at times to give up the task and take up some other crop. Such moments are his worst, for if he sticks to his one problem and endeavors to profit by his experience he will in the end succeed.

Coming back to the question of how violets are grown to-day, we find that those engaged in the work may be divided into two groups, (1) extensive or what may be called violet farmers, and (2) intensive or violet growers proper. Of course one will find numerous gradations, but for practical purposes they may be classed under the foregoing heads. Violet farming is often practiced in more or less remote country districts, where land and labor are cheap. Houses are seldom used for such work, but frames are resorted to, and the care of the plants is left to boys—sometimes colored, sometimes white—overlooked by the owner of the place or perhaps by a foreman or two. In a number of cases this method is practiced by women, and not without success. Of course there are numerous places where work of this kind could be carried on with a fair prospect of success. There are many farms seventy-five, one hundred, and even two hundred or three hundred miles from our large cities which with ordinary farm crops barely yield a living. In such cases a young or middle-aged person might take up this work and make it more profitable than the mere growing of farm crops. In all such cases, however, it must be borne in mind that to succeed there must be work night and day perhaps for a time, and while it may never be the heavy, killing labor which farm work is often made to be, it is ceaseless, tiresome toil just the same.

The intensive grower, on the other hand, should endeavor to locate within easy driving distance or shipping distance of his principal market; that is, he should if possible be located so that he can pick his flowers and have them in his dealer's hands within an hour or earlier if possible. It is the sweet, delicious fragrance that sells this flower and the moment it is picked it begins to lose this all-important thing. Therefore endeavor to locate so that you are in quick reach of your principal dealer, keeping constantly in mind the fact that your success depends largely on his success. Proximity to market should be set down as the first requisite to success, but not the only one by any means. Character of the soil, and facilities for obtaining manure, water, and other necessities must be considered. These factors will all be described in detail under their proper heads.

Last and most important of all, the man himself must be considered, or if possible must consider himself. No man can learn to grow violets from reading books, nor can he expect to get this knowledge from watching others. He can get help and suggestions of course, but the problems themselves he must work out alone. There is no such thing as luck in growing this crop, although it often looks that way. A man succeeds because he has the necessary knowledge to take advantage of the little things and make the most of them. Another fails because he does not see or fails to realize the importance of the little hourly and we might almost say minutely occurring things which are necessary to make the plants grow and thrive. It is not sufficient to be able to put on water, mix soil, to fire, or to feed and propagate the plants properly. The man may do all these according to the very best practices and yet his plants will never grow and bloom like those of the man who has the intuitive knowledge to realize the little needs and to make the cumulative effects of this knowledge felt in just the right way and at the right time. All this is hard to put into words, and will not be understood at all by some readers, but it is seen everywhere, from the lady who grows only a few house plants, but always succeeds with them, to the grower with his acres of glass in which every plant seems to spring into vigorous growth so long as his watchful eye is upon them and his hand is present to guide and direct the various operations.

The successful grower then is born, not made, for it is not a question of mechanics, but one of brains, and therefore, if there is not an inherent love for plants—that feeling of sympathy between them and you—some other work would better be undertaken. With love for the work and appreciation of every need of the plants, success will in the end result even though many difficulties in the way of surroundings must be overcome. To conclude, the whole gist of this argument is that surroundings, of course, count for considerable in such work, but more than all the rest success depends on the man himself, or rather on what he has in him. The man who truly succeeds in this work will succeed in almost any business, for all success really traces back to one thing, namely, ability to see, to grasp, and to utilize little things to the best advantage. Look after these and the big ones will look out for themselves.

CHAPTER II.

THE SOIL.

The soil forms the basis for all work in plant growth and it is proper therefore that it should be discussed first. Violets will grow on almost any soil, but to obtain the best results it is necessary to pay attention to certain important characters of the soil, particularly those relating to its physical properties. The importance of the relation of the physical properties of the soil, that is, texture, temperature, and moisture, to plant growth is not fully appreciated. By texture is meant the character of the particles which make up the soil, while structure has to do with the arrangement of these particles and their relation to each other. The particles, or grains, of which soils are composed vary greatly in size, and to distinguish them they have received certain conventional names, such as clay, fine silt, silt, fine sand, sand, etc. The clay particles are extremely minute, silt grains are larger, and so on until we have coarse sand or gravel, with grains $1/25$ to $1/12$ of an inch in diameter. Upon the amounts of the various constituents, i. e., clay, fine silt, silt, fine sand, etc., depends the porosity of the soil, the readiness with which the air penetrates it and water moves through it, its water-holding capacity, and finally its temperature.*

By varying the texture of the soil its water content is varied, its capacity for heat is modified, and so on until every important factor, including food, in the ordinary acceptance of the word, is involved. To these variations the plant adapts itself, and the result may be extensive leaf development with few or no flowers or vice versa, a weakened condition of the tissues (making the plant subject to the attacks of enemies, especially fungi), and so on through a list of other possibilities. To illustrate more fully, we may say that in our experience the Lady Hume Campbell violet seems to thrive best on relatively light soil, that is, a soil which contains a comparatively small amount of clay. The Marie Louise, on the other hand, does best with more clay, or in other words a heavier soil. The violet soils of the Poughkeepsie region contain from eight to fifteen per cent of clay, and it is here that the highest success is attained with this particular variety. In parts of Maryland and Virginia where the Campbell violet is grown extensively, the soils frequently contain six to eight per cent of clay, so that it will be seen that there is considerable difference as regards the structure of the two classes of soils. It follows,

---
*Galloway, B. T., Yearbook of the Department of Agriculture for 1895, p. 250.

of course, that where soils showing so much difference in structure are used the plants in each case have different sets of factors to which they must adapt themselves, and in doing this they may be so modified as to materially affect the development of the flowers.

Soils of both the heavy and moderately heavy types are found in many places and if they do not occur naturally the desired effects may be approximated by combinations of light and heavy soils. We have never found it satisfactory to lighten heavy soil by mixing in sand alone. This takes away the life of the soil and plants never succeed so well in it as when the desired conditions are produced by mixing a heavy and a light soil. For example, we may have in one part of a field a soil containing fifteen to twenty per cent of clay and in another one containing four or five per cent. By mixing these two soils in equal proportion a combination is effected which, other conditions being equal, will prove better for violets than either soil used alone.

Of course it must be remembered that the conditions for plants under glass are different from those out-of-doors. Outside the plant has to take what it can get in the way of water, air, and other important conditions for growth, while inside these are in a measure made to order by the grower himself. It follows, therefore, that even where the soil is not what it should be the grower has it within his power, to a large extent, to overcome the difficulties by a proper manipulation of the surroundings.

This question of the structure of the soil and its relation to plant growth is a rather difficult one to explain in words. The practical grower learns by experience how to judge a soil largely by its appearance and its "feel" when taken in the hand. The facts given in regard to the effects of structure of soil on plant growth, therefore, help a novice by acquainting him with matters he ought to know, but they will not show him what he can do, for experience alone can teach him this. Any soil that will grow a good crop of potatoes will, with proper manuring, grow good violets. This means that the soil should be a moderately heavy loam, that it should not pack or puddle readily, and that it should contain plenty of fibrous material, which can be obtained by using good turf or sod.

We prefer in all cases to use good sod or turf, cutting this not more than three or four inches thick. Where land is plentiful, that is, where the grower has several acres at his disposal, it will be best to keep part of it constantly in grass. Blue grass, white clover, and redtop make a good mixture. For every bushel of blue grass seed use one quart of white clover and one-third bushel of redtop. Coarse grasses, like orchard grass and timothy, should be avoided, as the stems and heavy roots are sources of annoyance in handling the soil. Where one has land that can be spared he should allow for every thousand plants not less than one-twentieth of an acre in grass upon which he can depend for soil. The soil after being used can be hauled out and after being spread on the ground be reseeded and in six or eight years will propably be as good as new. In the majority of cases it is necessary to purchase the soil and this is usually done through contractors and sometimes from farmers who have the sod to spare. It is customary to pay from seventy-five cents to one dollar per cubic yard for good sod cut three or four inches thick and delivered on the place. A cubic yard contains twenty-seven cubic feet, that is, a pile one foot high, three feet wide, and nine feet long. More often the soil is bought merely by the "load," a load being usually about a yard—sometimes a little more, sometimes less. Seventy-five cents to one dollar per load is the price usually paid for soil.

Some prefer to stack the soil, that is, to cut it and pile it in a heap in the early fall, but this is not always practicable, hence very often the work is left till spring. On the whole we can see no advantage in the early fall stacking unless it can be done during a time when work is not pressing. Where practicable our preference is to cut the sod in the fall and allow it to stand in the field unpiled until it has been frozen hard three or four times. In this way grubs, nematodes, and the larvæ of many insects are killed, and at the same time benefit is derived from the effects of the frost on the mechanical and chemical condition of the soil. Before hard winter weather sets in the soil should be either hauled close to the greenhouses and piled or else made into a heap where it stands. In sections where the soil is not from limestone formation, fresh slacked lime should be added to it when it is being put into the heap or directly after cutting. Lime should be added at the rate of about two-thirds of a bushel for each one thousand square feet cut. In stacking the soil we prefer to make a heap about four feet high, twenty to twenty-five feet wide, and of any length desired. At this time the manure, which should have been previously procured and put into good condition, is to be added to the soil. As a rule one part of manure to four parts of soil will make a combination sufficiently rich for any purpose. This is assuming, of course, that the manure is well rotted and free from light chaff and straw. Well-rotted cow manure is preferable if it can be obtained, but if not, well-rotted and carefully handled horse manure will answer equally as well. Avoid all experimenting with chemical fertilizers. They are well enough in their place, and in the hands of one who has had experience no harm will result from the use of a little pure, ground, undissolved bone, but it must be pure and applied at the rate of not more than one-half bushel for each one thousand plants. The bone should be mixed with the soil when the heap is being made. When a cart and horse are at hand we prefer to use them

4.—*Mixing soil. Spreading manure in layers between the soil.*

in making the heap. Four loads of soil, each a cubic yard, are hauled and spread, and then a load of manure is added and spread over the soil. This is continued until the first layer of the heap is of the desired width and length, when a second layer is formed in the same way. After finishing each

5.—*Mixing soil. Breaking and pulverizing the sod preparatory to putting it down with layers of manure.*

layer the bone meal may be sown thinly over the surface. Put it on about as thick as is done in sanding or sawdusting a floor. Working in this way, two active men can put into a heap forty to fifty yards of soil a day, or a sufficient quantity for four thousand to five thousand plants, figuring that the beds contain six inches of fresh made soil and that the manure and turf are one hundred to two hundred feet apart. It is seen, therefore, that each cubic yard of the mixture is sufficient for one hundred plants, allowing a depth of six inches for the beds.

When soil is purchased, or even when it is obtained from one's own place, it is never exactly alike any two years. For this reason it is a good plan to experiment a little before the general mixing is commenced. It takes very little time to make up several lots of soil in different proportions, using a water pail to make the measurements. For instance, we have soil from two localities, one of which is moderately heavy and the other light, and also well rotted manure which we make up in the following combinations:

(1) Light soil, one part.
Heavy soil, three parts.
Manure, one part.

(2) Light soil, two parts.
Heavy soil, two parts.
Manure, one part.

(3) Light soil, two parts.
Heavy soil, three parts.
Manure, one part.

(4) Heavy soil, four parts.
Manure, one part.

By using a pail, only small quantities of soil and manure are needed, but there will be sufficient material in each case after a thorough mixing to tell what the combinations look and feel like. It is always best to allow the heaps to stand a week or two for they often change their texture on standing, especially when lime is used. With a little practice one can soon determine in his own mind what combinations suit him best, and then he will at least have a rational basis to work upon.

Right here we may utter a word of warning against the growing practice of allowing the experimenting mania to get the better of judgment. Some individuals are over-inquiring, and for this reason the temptation is to experiment continually, with the result that nothing succeeds, for the simple reason that one thing is not tried long enough to find out its real value. We find a grower trying first this, then that fertilizer or method, with the result that by and by he gives up in disgust and says that his soil or his section is not suited to the crop he is attempting to grow. If he could only be brought to a realization of the fact that the trouble is not wholly in the soil or surroundings, but is partly in himself, he would soon be on the road to success. We have known men to spend years of work in experimenting one way or another, and at the end of that time they would be little wiser than when they commenced. All this time the plants have been doctored with insecticides and fungicides, fed on many kinds of food, and in short made to run the whole gamut of crank and quack notions advertised from time to time. What is needed here is a mind cure for the individual and less doctoring for the plants. Experiment, of course, but do not be led away by it, and do not allow every new idea or suggestion to take you from the main purpose or to bias your judgment.

To return from our digression, the soil when heaped should be protected by rough boards or by some other means from rains. Much benefit will result if the soil is turned two or three times before it is taken into the houses. Many omit this, but we are convinced that it pays to turn it as this improves its condition in many ways. The cost will not exceed fifty cents per thousand plants for each turning. Reference has been made to the quantity of soil used, but it is desirable to enter somewhat into detail upon this point. We aim to put in six inches of fresh soil each year. Plants may do well on less or even on the soil that has been used once, but the grower who is in the business for all there is to be made out of it, can not afford to run any risks, hence he should calculate on not less than six inches of new soil each year. To determine then how much soil is necessary, merely multiply the length of each bed in feet and inches by the width, and multiply this by one-half. This will give the number of cubic feet, and as there are twenty-seven cubic feet in a cubic yard, the number of cubic feet divided by twenty-seven will give the number of cubic yards. For example, it has been our practice to have our beds numbered (these numbers are held constant from year to year) as follows:

Bed No. 1. 75 x 6 feet=450 square feet x ½ foot=225 cubic feet, or practically 8 cubic yards.
Bed No. 2. 125 x 5 feet=625 square feet x ½ foot=312 cubic feet÷27=11.4 yards.

All the beds being numbered in this way it is an easy matter to tell just how much soil will be needed. Of course in considering the bulk as a whole the manure must be counted in, that is, if a total of one hundred yards of prepared soil is needed the manure will form one-fourth of this, or twenty-five yards. It will be necessary therefore to purchase seventy-five yards of soil proper and twenty-five yards of manure for the mixture. The cost of manure will of course depend on many circumstances, but in the vicinity of cities it can seldom be bought for less than seventy-five cents a cubic yard, or about two dollars and a half for a two-horse wagon load.

The foregoing statements in regard to soil, mixing, etc., are based upon the supposition that the grower is near a city, where land is high, and that his work is on an intensive plan, and further, that the plants are grown where they are to stand and not planted in the field and then moved in. No man who is in the business to compete with the best growers can afford to run the risk of growing his plants in the field and moving them into houses. From the time the cutting is made until the old plant is thrown away the work is or should be entirely under glass.

Where violet farming is practiced, i. e., where land is plentiful and the crop is grown in frames, it is customary in some sections to merely plow up a fresh piece of sod each year or every two or three years and move the frames. We do not recommend this practice and believe that it pays to bring the soil into heaps and mix it as described even if it is to be used in frames. The more the soil is handled the better, providing of course the work is not done when there is too much moisture present. Never allow a shovel to touch the soil when the latter is wet, for irreparable injury can be done at such a time. Wait until the soil is mealy and never touch it when it is pasty and putty-like to the touch. It must be remembered that the soil is not a dead, inert mass, but is an exceedingly complicated material—an active working laboratory, teeming with life and performing functions which we as yet but little understand. Fortunate is the man who knows enough to appreciate this fact and to let the soil alone when by so doing its wonderful mechanism is brought into play for the best use of the plants it sustains.

CHAPTER III.

CONSTRUCTION OF HOUSES AND FRAMES.

CONSTRUCTION OF HOUSES.

Probably more makeshifts in the way of houses for growing violets have been used in this country than for any other crop. The evolution of this part of the work has been exceptionally slow, so that it is difficult to find at this time a thoroughly modern establishment in every way. Ordinary cold frames were first used; then in order to get at the plants in bad weather a pit was made so as to obtain head room and still utilize the sash and keep the plants near the glass. Gradually growers began to get their plants above ground and to increase the amount of head room and air space by raising the sash above the beds. Many houses are still made on this plan, while a comparatively few are built with stationary sash bars and permanent glass roof. There are no special advantages in making a house of sash, except in certain cases, which will be mentioned later. Such houses cannot be made wind or water-tight, and as a rule are so full of wood as to be unnecessarily dark. When it was considered necessary to take the glass off in summer, sashes,

44 CONSTRUCTION.

6.—*Sash house with sash off.*

of course, were an important item, for they could easily be removed and stored until wanted in the fall. If one intends to make a permanent house we by all means recommend the fixed roof, with

7.—*House twelve feet wide, six feet to ridge; side ventilators of glass. This is one of a block of five houses, each seventy-five feet long.*

ventilators and other necessary adjuncts arranged as we shall now proceed to describe.

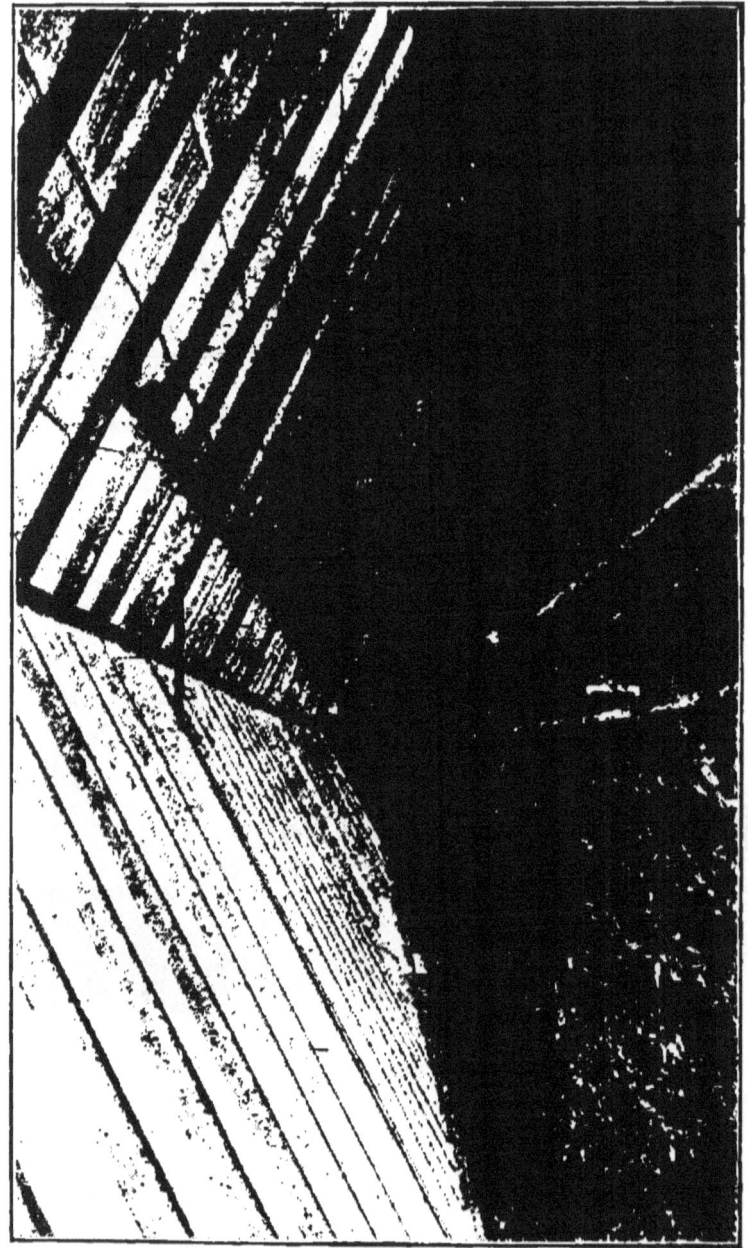

8.—Type of even span house, twelve feet wide, showing method of running heating pipes and constructing beds. Flow pipe in ridge.

All things considered, our preference is for even span houses running north and south. The violet does not thrive well under glaring sunlight. It needs light, but this should be softened and diffused in order to insure the best results in the growth and the size and color of the flowers. The three-quarter span house facing south is apt to be too bright, and if heavy shading is resorted to it is effective in bright weather but makes it too dark when cloudy. Economy in space and economy in building, furthermore, can be attained by adopting the even span north and south style of house. In our work we have made it a point to keep a careful record of not only the flowers from each kind of house, but from each bed in a house. These records, kept from year to year, furnish interesting information and enable one who is looking to every detail to make changes that will result to his advantage. The three-quarter span house facing south in our case never gave as many flowers per square foot of bed space by twenty to twenty-five per cent as the even span houses running north and south.

When capital and space are limited we know of no better style of house than a narrow, plain, even span, built on the ridge and furrow plan, and running north and south. The length may be from seventy-five to one hundred and fifty feet.

Our preference is for houses one hundred feet long, twelve feet wide, seven feet to the ridge

48　CONSTRUCTION.

9.—Type of even span house, twelve feet wide, with two deep walks, showing heating pipes, and method of constructing beds, roofs, and ends.

HOUSES. 49

from the bottom of the walk, and two feet eight inches high on the sides above ground level (see figure 8). Where the amount of ground is limited these houses may be built together—two, three,

10.—*Shed at north end of houses, showing method of construction. Shed has glass roof.*

five, or seven, as the case may be—without intervening walls. At the north end of the houses and running the entire length across the ends there should be a lean-to shed eight feet wide and provided with glass roof sloping to the north. Against the north wall may be placed a propagating bed three and one-half feet wide, leaving four and one-half feet clear space for a walk and entrance to each house. If more than six

11.—*Interior of shed shown in 10. Propagating bench on the right, supply pipes (two inch) on the left, shed eight feet wide.*

houses are in the block, the boiler should be placed near the center in a pit dug beneath the shed. If necessary, of course, the entire space beneath the shed may be devoted to coal, a workshop, and perhaps a place for tools. If the number of houses are three or less, the boiler may be placed at one end of the shed in a pit, as already described. The end selected should depend upon

12—Roofs of twelve foot houses, showing method of construction and of attaching ventilators; one row of glass between the ventilators.

the general slope of the land, the object being to get the boiler at the lowest point. Following is a detailed statement in regard to the points to consider in this type of house:

> Length, one hundred feet, with one foot fall to carry off water.
> Inside width, twelve feet.
> Height to ridge from bottom of walk, seven feet.
> Height of side from top of plate to bottom of gutter, twenty inches (see figure 24).
> Walls below plates to be boarded up with rough lumber first, then covered with rustic siding (see figure 24).
> Number of walks, one in each house, placed in the center.
> Width of walk, fourteen inches.
> Depth of walk, twelve inches.
> Number of beds, two.
> Width of each bed, five feet five inches.
> Depth of beds, twelve inches.
> Posts in outside walls, four by four inches sawed cedar, chestnut, or locust, set four feet apart center to center, and two and one-half feet in the ground.
> Posts in inside walls, four by four inches, set eight feet apart center to center, and two and one-half feet in the ground.
> Gutters, three piece, six inches in the clear, made of two inch clear cypress (see figure 18).
> Wall plates, two by eight inch clear cypress, to be notched around posts.
> Gable plates for end of each house, two by eight inch clear cypress.
> Gable rafters, one and three-quarters by two and one-quarter inch clear cypress.
> Sash bars clear cypress, one and one-quarter by two and one-half inches, with drip groove, all bars to extend from gutter to ridge.
> Rafters, two by four inch, clear cypress, to be set every sixteen feet. Rafters to take place of sash bar.
> Ridge (with ridge cap), two by six inches.
> Top ventilators, two by four feet, or made to cover three rows of glass set fifteen inches, including sash bars. One row of glass to be left between the ventilators.

Headers to be placed under ventilator.

Ventilators on side, two by four feet, continuous, and to lap on post one-half.

Glass ten by fifteen inches, double thick, second quality, lapped and bedded in putty. Glass set fifteen inch way.

South ends of houses glass, with exception of door, which should be four feet wide so as to admit a wheelbarrow readily.

North ends of houses opening into shed to be made of tongue and groove pine, with doors the same size as those on south end.

Walls of shed to be made of rustic siding nailed to two by four studs set eighteen inches apart. Inside of shed to be lined with tongue and groove yellow pine.

Wall plate of shed, two by six yellow pine.

Top plate of shed, same as wall plate.

Doors in north wall of shed, four feet wide, opening opposite doors in north end of houses.

Posts for sides of beds, two by four hemlock, set four feet apart, and wired to opposite posts or to stakes to prevent spreading. Set wires ten inches below top of bed.

Sides of beds, one by twelve inch hemlock boards nailed to outside of the two by four posts.

Heating pipes, black wrought iron screw joints, two one and one-half inch flows for each house and ten one and one-quarter inch returns (five on each side of house). Pipes run so that the highest point, including expansion tank, is directly over the boiler.

Flow and returns in all houses to have the same fall, i. e., about one inch for every ten feet of pipe.

To feed five houses of the size here given (twelve by one hundred feet), it will be necessary to run out two two and one-half inch pipes from the boiler, allowing one pipe to feed the two houses on the west and one to feed the three on the east. The west is given the advantage on account of the greater exposure.

Top ventilators operated by plain lifting rods with holes and pins to give a four to sixteen inch opening.

54 CONSTRUCTION.

The accompanying illustrations will make plain the points mentioned.

The second type of house, which will require

13.—*A twelve foot house, showing method of constructing and attaching side ventilators.*

more ground and capital, is also even span, running north and south, but with a space of eight feet between the houses. Following are the principal features of this style of house:

Length of house, one hundred feet, with one foot fall to carry off water.

Width of shed at north end, ten feet.

Width of house inside, twenty-four feet.

Height of walls from top of plate to bottom of gutter, twenty inches. Plate to be twelve inches above grade (see figure 24).

Walls below plate to be boarded up with rough lumber and then covered with rustic siding (see figure 24).

Height of house inside from top of center bed to bottom of ridge, nine feet.

Number of walks, two.

Width of walks each, fourteen inches.

Number of beds, three.

Width of center bed, ten feet ten inches.

Width of side beds each, five feet five inches.

Depth of beds, twelve inches.

Posts in side walls, sawed cedar, chestnut, or locust, four by four inches, set four feet apart center to center and two and one-half feet in the ground.

Gutters, three piece cypress, six inches in the clear (see figure 18).

Plates, two by eight inches, clear cypress, cut to fit around posts and to receive bottom of ventilator.

Gable plates at ends of house, two by eight inches clear cypress.

Gable rafters, one and three-quarters by two and one-quarter inches clear cypress.

Purlins, one inch black pipe, run under each slope five feet nine inches from ridge.

Supports for purlins, one inch pipe, long enough to extend through bed and into cement block in the ground.

Support for ridge, one and one-quarter inch black pipe, placed eight feet apart and set the same as supports under purlins.

Iron posts, to be attached to purlins by T's one and one-quarter inch through, so as to slip over purlin pipe, with one inch side to take support.

Sash bars, clear cypress, one and one-quarter by two and one-half inches, with drip groove, all bars to extend from gutter to ridge.

Rafters, none.

Ridge, clear cypress, two by six inches, with ridge cap.

Top ventilators on both sides, each ventilator two by four feet, or long enough to cover three sash bars and glass, leaving one row of glass between each two ventilators, headers under ventilators.

Ventilators on sides, two by four feet, continuous, and made to lap on posts.

Ventilator-raising apparatus for top and sides consisting of geared wheels, shafts, arms, and rods.

Glass, ten by fifteen inches, double thick, second quality, lapped, and bedded in putty.

Posts for supporting sides of beds, two by four inch hemlock, set four feet apart and wired to opposite posts to prevent bed from spreading.

Sides of beds, one inch hemlock or cypress, nailed to outside of posts.

Heating pipes, black wrought iron and screw joint, being run so that the highest point is directly over the boiler.

Flow pipe, two and one-half inches, to be carried directly under the ridge and to fall to south end about one inch in every ten feet.

Returns, twelve one and one-half inch pipe, to fall one inch in ten feet from south to north end, two pipes to be carried over center bed and five along each wall. This will give sufficient radiating surface to maintain with hot water an inside temperature of fifty degrees F. with an outside temperature at zero and no wind blowing. Plugged openings should be left for at least four additional returns so as to be on the safe side. This can be done with very little additional expense and may be worth a good many dollars at some future time.

As many houses as may be desired can be built after this plan, all connecting at the north end with the shed having a slope running to the north, the same as described for the first style of house. It is best to leave at least eight feet between each two houses to faclitate ventilation, the taking out of plants and soil, clearing off the snow from the roofs, and other necessary work.

So much for the main points involved in the construction of the two principal styles of houses. In the matter of heating we have considered only hot water, as we believe it has advantages over steam in growing violets. A proper boiler is of

14.—*Fastening pipes to posts by tin clips.*   15.—*Fastening pipes to posts by bent wire nails.*

the utmost importance—so important in fact that the most careful consideration should be given to its selection. Notwithstanding all that has been written on heating it is a fact that nearly every man who goes into greenhouse work is dissatisfied until he has spent a good deal of money and time in experimenting on this feature. Experience obtained in this way is sometimes dearly bought and it pays

16.—Interior of twelve foot house, showing method of constructing south end and door.

better to take the advice of others who have gone over the same ground and have reached conclusions that will apply to your case.

HEATING. 59

Boiler makers, under the stimulus of competition, have, in many cases, wandered away from the simple principles that must be considered in making an economical, efficient apparatus. In

17.—*Interior of house, showing method of connecting flow pipe with four returns.*

our experience with boilers we have never found any that would fill all requirements so nearly as one of simple construction, giving the largest

60   CONSTRUCTION.

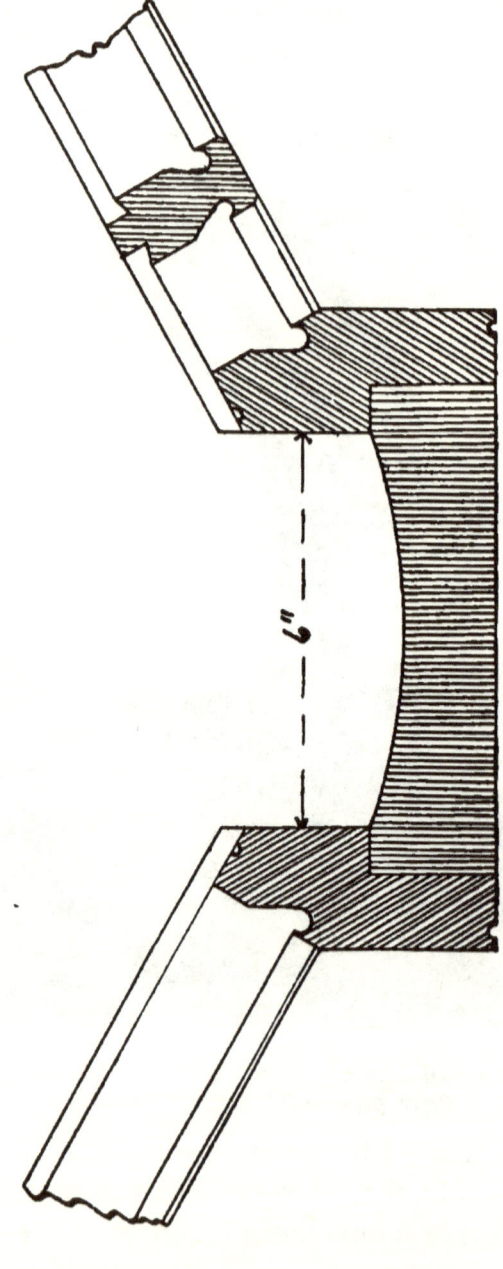

18.—Ridge and furrow house construction. Method of making gutter and attaching sash bar; drip groove in gutter to carry off water inside; drip groove in sash bar; three-piece gutter, six inches in the clear, stock make and size.

possible amount of direct heating surface, and offering the least resistance to the movement of the water, and a fire box deep and big enough to carry a large amount of fuel at slow combustion.

19.—*Interior construction. Method of connecting returns at north end of house.*

There is no economy in curtailing the size of the fire box and adding sections, which at best can only receive the hot gases. In order to get the

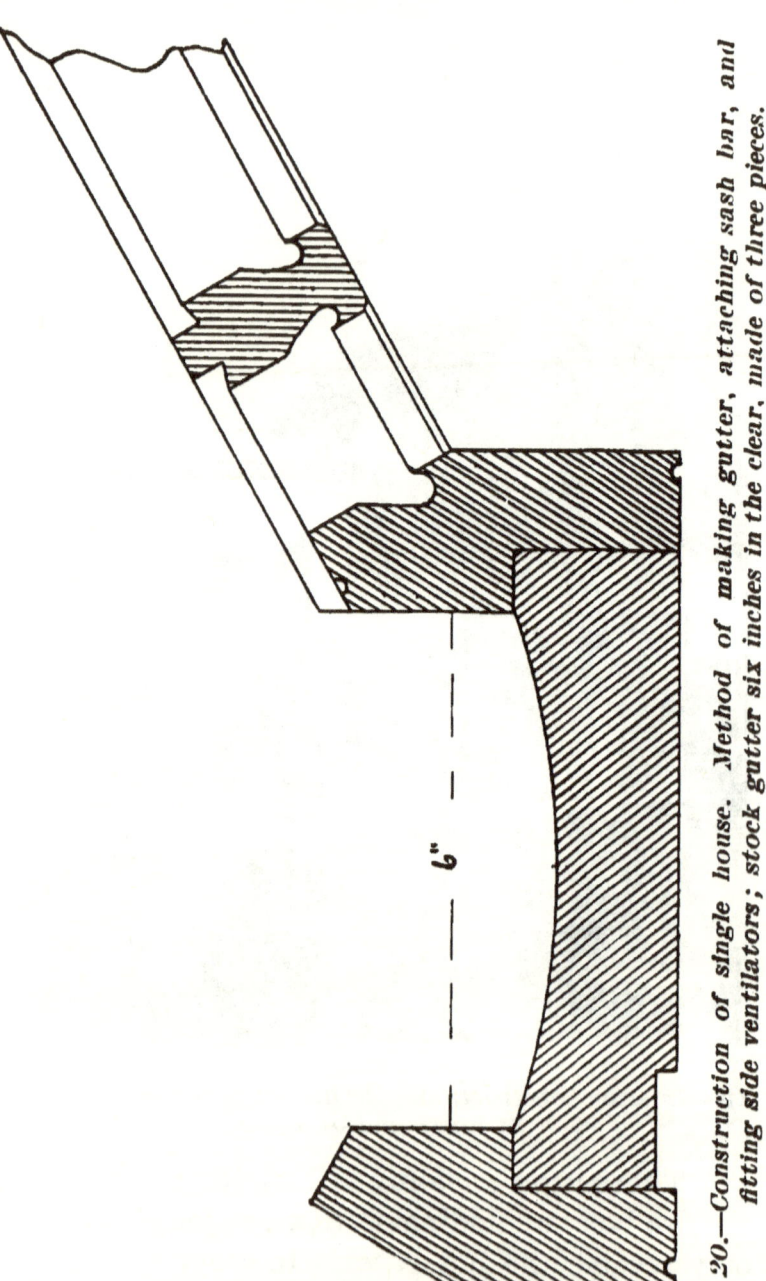

20.—Construction of single house. Method of making gutter, attaching sash bar, and fitting side ventilators; stock gutter six inches in the clear, made of three pieces.

full service out of such a boiler it will be necessary to carry a hot fire, and as a result a large per cent of the heat goes up the chimney. Boilers, therefore, should be selected with due regard to (1) the amount of direct heating surface, (2) perpendicular circulation of the water in the boiler, (3) the capacity for fuel, and (4) conveniences in the matter of suitable grates, drafts, and doors. Most boilers are rated on the number of square feet of pipe they will heat. As a rule, at least twenty-five per cent margin should be allowed on these figures in order to be on the safe side. For example, if a boiler is rated to heat one thousand square feet of pipe it should not have more than seven hundred or seven hundred and fifty feet put upon it. It may heat the thousand feet at a pinch, but the grower wants it to heat the pipe at all times with a slow fire that will stand without attention at least six or seven hours.

The saddle, conical, and locomotive types of boilers are probably as efficient as any we now have, and by taking any one of these and fitting it up with the modern improvements in the way of deep fire box, grates, ash-pit, door and flue drafts, and dampers, it would, in all probability, do the work more economically and efficiently than a large number of the intricate forms now on the market. There is the keenest competition among boiler makers, and as a rule, they are to be

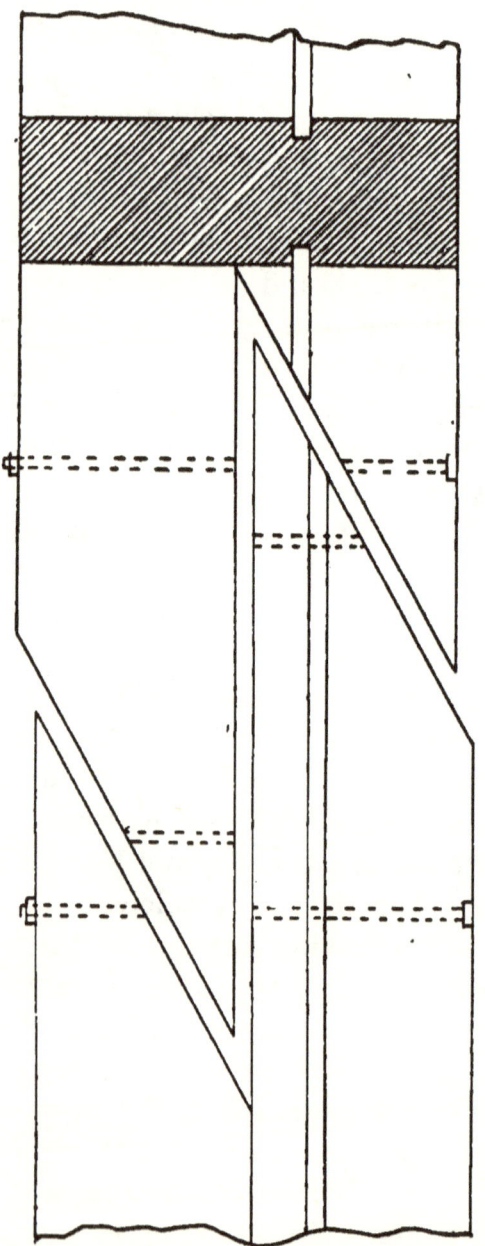

21.—Method of splicing ridge.

HEATING. 65

commended for the great energy they show in endeavoring to adapt their apparatus to the demands of the trade. Prices are so close that every additional ounce of iron counts, and for this reason it would seem to be the part of wisdom to

22.—*House twenty-four feet wide; posts set and shed at north end built first.*

simplify construction as much as possible. It is a matter of theoretical calculation to determine what each section will do when added to a boiler. In practice, however, it is frequently found that each section beyond reach of direct fire contact utterly fails to do what in theory it ought to accomplish. Good boilers made by responsible firms are within the reach of all nowadays and it

23.—*Constructing house twenty-four feet wide; second step, making beds and walks.*

hardly pays, therefore, to attempt to make them out of coils of pipe. By the time the pipe is purchased, put together, and bricked up, and the doors, grates, drafts, and other necessary conveniences obtained, the cost is nearly as great as when a first-class boiler, ready to set up and start off, is purchased.

As to the cost of boilers, it may be said that for

24.—*Constructing house twenty-four feet wide; third step, running gutters and notching plate around posts.*

every five hundred square feet of pipe it will cost seventy-five dollars for boiler capacity to heat it, or fifteen dollars for every hundred square feet of heating surface. Therefore to heat a house such as described, namely, twelve by one hundred feet and seven feet to ridge, the boiler would cost seventy five dollars. For each additional house of the same length joined to the next without partition walls, an additional fifty dollars should be added for boiler capacity. To heat a house one hundred feet long and twenty-four feet wide, such as described as the second type, would require a boiler costing one hundred and twenty-five dollars. For each additional house separated from the other by an alley of eight feet, it would require seventy-five dollars additional for boiler capacity. When the amount of pipe to heat exceeds twenty-five hundred square feet it is best to have more than one boiler—in fact it is a question whether it is not best in all cases to have boilers so arranged that there is a reserve on hand for emergencies, which may arise at any time. It is also a question as to whether it would not pay to have a night fireman in all cases where the number of plants exceeds ten thousand.

This brings us to a consideration of the total cost of the types of houses described. Taking one hundred feet as the length, a house twelve feet wide and seven feet to the ridge, with a twenty inch opening on sides, would cost as follows:

40 posts for side walls, 4 x 4 inches, 6 or 7 feet long, at 35 cents each	$14 00
205 lineal feet 3-piece gutter, 6 inches in clear, at $16.20 per 100 feet	33 21

COST OF HOUSES.

1200 lineal feet of sash bars, 1½ x 2¼ inches, in 14 foot lengths, at $1.50 per 100 feet..................	$18 00
225 lineal feet 2 x 8 inch wall plate for sides and ends, at $7.20 per 100 feet.....................	16 20
96 lineal feet 2 x 4 inch rafters, 14 foot lengths, at $4.00 per 100 feet...	3 84
64 lineal feet of gable rafters, 1¾ x 2¼, at $2.36 per 100 feet...	1 51
112 lineal feet of 2 x 6 inch ridge, at $5.40 per 100 feet...	6 05
100 lineal feet of ridge cap, 1¼ x 3½, at $2.20 per 100 feet..	2 20
20 top ventilators, each 2 x 4 feet, at 40 cents each (5 cents per square foot)..........................	8 00
75 lineal feet of headers for ventilators, at 4 cents per foot..	3 40
50 side ventilators, 2 x 4 feet, at 40 cents each....	20 00
52 hemlock posts 2 x 4 inches, for sides of beds, each post 3 feet long, at 4 cents each..........	2 08
200 lineal feet hemlock boards, 12 x 1 inch, at $1.60 per 100 feet, for sides of beds.....................	3 20
600 board feet rough hemlock for walls below plate, at $1.50 per 100................................	9 00
300 board feet rustic siding, at $1.40 per 100.........	4 20
140 pairs 3 inch strap hinges for ventilators, with screws, at 5 cents each.............................	7 00
20 plain lifting rods for top ventilators, with plate, staple, and pin, each rod 16 inches long, made of ¾ inch strap iron, at 6 cents each...	1 20
50 ventilator fasteners for side ventilators, at 8 cents each...	4 00
1100 feet of 1¼ inch wrought iron heating pipe, 10 returns, at 6 cents a foot............................	66 00
225 feet 1½ inch pipe for flows, at 8 cents a foot..	18 00
4 manifolds, five 1¼ inch openings on side and one 1½ inch opening at each end, at 65 cents each...	2 60
2 1½ inch long screws, at 30 cents each.............	60
10 1¼ inch long screws, at 25 cents each............	2 50
Fittings..	4 00

1 hot water boiler, complete and set ready for connection, including 8 inch chimney of terra cotta pipe...	$75 00
50 feet tongue and groove yellow pine for two doors, at $2.00 per 100 feet.......................	1 00
Shed at north end of house to cover boiler pit, 12 feet long, 8 feet wide, 8 feet high in front, 6 feet at back, with one door and boiler pit, complete.......................................	40 00
100 pounds of white lead, at 5 cents per pound....	5 00
5 gallons of linseed oil, with drier, at 65 cents per gallon...	3 25
100 pounds of putty, at 3 cents per pound..........	3 00
Nails and hardware.......................................	4 00
30 boxes 10 x 15 glass, double thick, second quality, at $2.25 per box..........................	67 50
8 boxes 14 x 16 glass for ventilators, at $2.75 per box..	22 00
Water pipes, including 1 inch main and ¾ inch branches for spigots...............................	12 00
Labor, including all carpenter work, painting, pipe fitting, setting boiler, etc.................	125 00
Freight, etc...	50 00
Total...$658 54	

In reference to labor, it may be said that it is necessarily one of the most difficult things to estimate. The house can be put up complete by one man with a laborer as a helper in twenty-five days or less. This would reduce the cost of labor to less than one hundred dollars. The amount estimated therefore is over rather than under what the actual cost ought to be.

The cost of the second type of house—one hundred by twenty-four feet—is as follows:

52 posts, 4 x 4 inches, 6 or 7 feet long, at 35 cents each...	$18 20

COST OF HOUSES.

205 lineal feet of gutter, at $16.20 per 100 feet.....	$33 21
650 board feet rough hemlock for sides and ends below plates, at $1.50 per 100 feet..............	9 75
300 board feet rustic siding, at $1.40 per 100 feet..	4 20
2400 lineal feet of sash bars in 14 foot lengths, at $1.50 per 100 feet......................	36 00
225 lineal feet, 2 x 8 inch wall plate, at $7.20 per 100 feet................................	16 20
54 lineal feet of gable rafters, at 2$\frac{3}{10}$ cents per foot	1 24
112 feet 2 x 6 ridge, at $5.40 per 100 feet..............	6 05
40 top ventilators, each 2 x 4 feet, at 40 cents each......................................	16 00
50 side ventilators, each 2 x 4 feet, at 40 cents each......................................	20 00
150 feet headers for top ventilators, at 4 cents per foot...................................	6 00
600 board feet hemlock boards for sides of beds, at $1.60 per 100 feet.....................	9 60
200 2 x 4 inch hemlock posts for sides of beds, at 5 cents each...............................	10 00
90 pairs of hinges, with screws, for ventilators, at 5 cents per pair with screws..................	4 50
Ventilating machinery, complete..................	100 00
1400 feet 1½ inch heating pipe, at 8 cents per foot..	112 00
125 feet 2½ inch heating pipe, at 15 cents per foot	18 75
4 manifolds, 1½ inch all round, at 75 cents each	3 00
Long screws and other fittings......................	15 00
400 feet of 1 inch pipe for purlins and purlin supports, at 5 cents per foot..........................	20 00
150 feet 1¼ inch pipe for ridge supports, at 6 cents per foot.................................	9 00
Fittings, including T's, for purlins and supports.....................................	12 00
1 boiler, complete and set, including 12 inch iron or terra cotta chimney........................	150 00
2 doors, at $2.00 each.....................................	4 00
Shed at north end of house, 10 feet wide, with glass roof as already described, including boiler pit boarded up.............................	100 00
300 pounds of white lead, at 5 cents per pound....	15 00

10 gallons linseed oil, with drier, at 65 cents per gallon.. 6 50
200 pounds of putty, at 3 cents per pound......... 6 00
Nails and hardware...................................... 15 00
60 boxes 10 x 15 glass, at $2.25 per box............. 135 00
10 boxes 14 x 16 glass for ventilators, at $2.75 per box.. 27 50
Water pipes including two 1 inch mains and ¾ inch laterals, with spigots 25 00
Labor for carpenter work, painting, and pipe fitting, complete.. 250 00
Freight, etc... 75 00

Total...$1289 70

25.—*Construction. Putting up the roof.*

We have already referred to houses made of

sash. For certain purposes houses of this kind will be found very useful, and it is important, therefore, to have sash on hand. Sash houses can be erected quickly and can be taken down when necessary and the sash themselves stored. A sash house is particularly valuable for wintering cuttings and taking care of them when made in spring. Furthermore, a house of this kind will be found very useful for growing reserve plants during the summer. It is always important to have on hand a supply of good plants to transplant where others are lost from the main houses. A sash house, constructed with open sides and ends, can be used for growing plants, and the latter will in such cases do much better than when grown in frames or in the open air. In the spring, however, when the main houses become crowded with boxes of cuttings, the sash house will be found exceedingly valuable for storing the flats of young plants. In such cases comparatively little heat is required, owing to the lateness of the season. The young plants are at all times within reach, so that they can be kept clean and fumigated with gas if it is found necessary to do so.

For houses of this character three by six sash are the most advantageous. Such sash made of white pine can be bought complete, that is, glazed and with two coats of paint, for two dollars each. The woodwork necessary for the construction of such a house would cost comparatively little. Ordinarily in constructing a house of this kind two beds are first made, with a walk fourteen inches wide between them. These beds are made of twelve inch hemlock boards, which are nailed to two by three inch hemlock posts set four feet apart. In order to keep the boards in place the hemlock posts are driven six to eight inches in the ground and then wired to opposite posts or to sticks driven down for the purpose. The total width of such a house should be ten feet, including the path. The path being fourteen inches wide, there is left on each side a bed four feet five inches wide. To support the sash, uprights, made of two by four hemlock studs, are nailed to the outside boards of the frame. These uprights are placed about six feet apart and should project two feet above the frame. After being set in this way and nailed to the boards, the tops should be sawed at the same slant or pitch the roof is to have. A two by three stud is then nailed to the tops of the posts for a plate and upon this the ends of the sash are allowed to rest. The sash are simply brought together at the top and nailed, no ridge being required. They are also nailed at the bottom and no further support is necessary.

Where the house is intended for late spring and summer use it is of course not necessary to provide for ventilation, as plenty of air is always circulating through the sides and ends, which are left open. For cuttings in the spring, however, where some heat is necessary, the sides and ends must be closed up. This can be done by means of rough pine or hemlock boards, over which may be nailed, on the outside, tarred paper. The ends may be closed in the same way, leaving a door at one end for entrance. In such cases it is necessary to effect ventilation to loosen about every third sash and hinge it at the top. Pieces of leather can be used for hinges and each sash may be raised and propped with a stick. A house of this kind sixty feet long should have on each side four movable sash for ventilating. The ventilating sash should not come opposite each other, otherwise they cannot be hinged at the top.

In order to heat a house of this kind for spring use, run two one and one-quarter inch pipes down each side, to be fed by a one and one-half inch flow running under the ridge or down the sash so as to get the proper fall. Such a house may be used for growing the violets through the season and is one of the most inexpensive that could be erected. In such a case, however, it will be necessary to run at least four one and one-quarter inch pipes down each side, the same to be fed by two one and one-half inch flows.

Such a house for spring use sixty feet in length, would cost approximately as follows:

40 sash, 3 x 6 feet, at $2.00 each............................	$80 00
Lumber for sides, ends, and beds...........................	20 00
Nails, hardware, etc.	2 00
Heating pipes and heating apparatus	50 00
Total	$152 00

76   CONSTRUCTION.

26.—Temporary house, made of sash nailed together at the top, supporting posts two by three inches.

As will be seen, this is a very cheap house, and will hold from forty to fifty thousand cuttings placed in flats. If planted in the ordinary way, i. e., eight by nine inches, it will hold about one thousand plants. For summer use alone, that is, without heating apparatus, sides, or ends, the house can be erected for less than one hundred dollars. For growing plants in order to get flowers throughout the winter the cost will be about two hundred dollars, on account of the extra heating pipe needed.

If a shorter house than the one here described is wanted it is a comparatively easy matter to build it. A house thirty feet long would cost little more than half as much, so it will be seen that there are a number of advantages in having sash for use in this way.

CONSTRUCTION OF FRAMES.

The simplest form of structure for growing violets is the frame, which may be either cold or heated. Frames should be located on ground that is well drained, and if possible should have some protection from north winds. It is customary to place them, when practicable, at the foot of a hill, but if this cannot be done it is desirable to have them on the windward side of trees or some similar place where the north wind will not sweep over them.

For violets the frames are ordinarily made on

78   CONSTRUCTION

27.—Simple cold frame, six feet wide and continuous

top of the ground, that is, it is best not to dig the ground out, for the reason that water is apt to accumulate around the roots and the plants in consequence will suffer. Rough pine boards are used for constructing the frames. The back of the frame is usually made of a board twelve inches wide, while for the front a board eight inches wide is required. Frames always face the south, that is, they run east and west. The frames may be made either continuous or in sections. When continuous, posts are driven into the ground and boards are nailed to them, so that the frame is just wide enough to take a sash six feet long. The length may be indefinite and will vary according to the surroundings and nature of the land. Ordinarily it is preferable to have several lengths of frames separated by six or eight feet rather than to have one long tier. After the boards have been erected they should be braced every six feet by a one by three inch strip sunk and nailed into the back and front boards level with the edge of each. Frames so constructed will cost about seventy-five cents per running foot. This is without mats or shutters for protecting the plants in very cold weather.

Mats may be made of straw or burlaps, and shutters may be constructed of wood, or if not made into the size of the sash themselves ordinary twelve foot boards can be used. For burlap mats or boards the additional cost of frame will be about fifteen cents per running foot, which makes

28.—Violets in frame, covered with lath screen.

FRAMES.

the total cost ninety cents per foot. Therefore a frame one hundred feet long, constructed as described, with mats or boards for covering in cold weather, will cost approximately ninety dollars. Such a frame will hold about twelve hundred plants, so that the cost of space per plant in this case will be approximately eight cents. As will be seen, this is the cheapest method for growing plants, and for this reason many adopt it in the beginning. There are so many disadvantages in growing plants in frames however, that they should not be used where it is possible to make a house. The disadvantages are referred to in detail in other places, so that it is not necessary to name them here.

The question of mats or of some means of protection during excessively cold weather is of great importance, for unless such protection is given the plants will be so severely frozen as to be made useless. The backs and fronts of the frames must also be protected as soon as cold weather sets in. This is usually accomplished by banking up soil or manure to within an inch or an inch and a half of the top of the frame. The most common practice for protecting the plants is using ordinary boards twelve inches wide and sixteen feet long. These are simply laid on the frames when cold weather comes on and serve in a measure to exclude the frost. It is much work, however, to put these boards on and take them off, for this

82 CONSTRUCTION.

29.—Violets in heated frames shaded by rough boards five feet above beds.

must be done promptly whenever the conditions require change. Mats are somewhat more convenient and are used to a considerable extent in various parts of the country. The cheapest, and in some respects the best form of mat is made of ordinary burlap quilted so as to hold between each piece about two inches of straw. The mats are ordinarily made of what is known as twelve ounce burlaps, forty-five inches wide, which costs about six cents a yard. The straw between the tackings of the mat is about two inches thick, but where the tackings are made it is only about half an inch thick, as the string is pulled tight and tied in a square knot to prevent all danger of its getting loose. These mats complete cost about thirty-five cents each, and with ordinary wear and tear will last two seasons. Mats similar to these are now offered by many seed dealers at very reasonable prices, so that it hardly pays to make them at home. Straw mats are also used to a considerable extent, but they are more expensive than the others, and with the handling they must necessarily get will not last very much longer.

Mats are in all cases preferable to boards. They keep the plants warmer and are not so unhandy to move about. The boards soon warp, and for this reason will not lie close to the glass. They are furthermore constantly in the way when laid between the frames, and as a rule cannot be handled readily by one person. Where frames

84 CONSTRUCTION.

30.—Violets in heated frames. Summer shading by boards; boiler house in the foreground.

are made in sections it is the practice to have each section long enough to take five sash. Usually a space of twelve or fifteen inches is left between each section. In summer the sash are taken off and the frames are stored where the weather will not affect them. There is no particular advantage in making frames in this way.

Frames are occasionally heated by means of hot water or steam pipes, and in this way the frost is excluded. The ordinary practice in heating with hot water is to run one one and a quarter inch pipe completely around the frame. The boiler is placed at a point several feet lower than the frame, and the pipe from this is so run as to give a slight rise to the end of the frame farthest from the boiler and a slight fall from the far end back to the boiler. The flow pipe is usually placed against the board on the north side of the frame, while the return is run along the board on the south side.

A boiler with sufficient pipe to heat a frame one hundred feet long and six feet wide will cost approximately fifty dollars. While there are some advantages in heating frames in this way it is a question whether it would not pay in the end to use the boiler in heating a house made of sash, as already described—that is, having the sash and the boiler, better results could probably be obtained by constructing a house of sash so that the plants would be accessible at all times and there would be no delay or trouble in case of bad weather or heavy snow.

A summarized comparison of the cost of the different structures described is interesting, and is, in round numbers, approximately as follows:

For the first type of house, 100 x 12 feet—
- Per running foot.. $7 00
- Per square foot of bed space............................. 63
- Per plant grown (2000 plants in each house)........ 32

For the second type of house, 100 x 24 feet—
- Per running foot.. 12 00
- Per square foot of bed space............................. 54
- Per plant (4000 plants in each house) 27

For a sash house, 60 x 10 feet—
- Per running foot.. 3 25
- Per square foot of bed space............................. 38
- Per plant... 19

For a cold frame, with mats of straw—
- Per running foot.. 90
- Per square foot of bed space............................. 8
- Per plant... 4

For heated frame—
- Per running foot.. 1 40
- Per square foot of bed space............................. 12
- Per plant... 6

It will be seen that of the two types of houses the larger one is proportionally the cheaper. It also has other advantages, the most important being that crops such as roses and carnations, may, with some minor changes, be grown in it. The low type of house, on the other hand, is not well adapted to the growth of any crop but the violet. In all cases there would be a saving where more

COST OF HOUSES.

than one house is built. In the case of the one hundred by twelve foot house, without intervening walls—

    3 can be erected complete for..................................$1,600
    5 can be erected complete for.................................. 2,100

There is not so much difference in the one hundred by twenty-four foot house—

    3 can be erected complete for..................................$2,700
    5 (with a capacity for 20,000 plants) can be erected complete for.. 4,200

CHAPTER IV.

WATER SUPPLY.

An abundant supply of good water is essential to the successful cultivation of any plant and the violet is no exception to this rule. Water is needed not only to keep the ground moist, but to syringe or spray in order to keep down red spider. For ordinary watering no force is required, but for spraying, arrangements must be made to get a pressure of not less than twenty pounds to the square inch in the system of pipes. Where city water is to be obtained and the rates are reasonable, the simplest plan is of course to merely get proper connections with the mains. Where this is not practicable, however, the water must be obtained either from wells or from some other source, and must be stored in a tank or some suitable reservoir to be drawn upon when wanted. For two to three thousand plants a tank of one thousand gallons capacity will be sufficient, and for every two thousand additional plants a thousand gallons more of reservoir space will be required. Thus for ten thousand plants a tank holding not less than five thousand gallons should be at hand. These statements apply mainly where windmills are used for pumping, but they will also hold good for almost any kind of a pumping plant, as allowance must always be made for breakdowns and other accidents.

A windmill offers the cheapest power for raising water, but its chief drawback is the uncertainty of its action. With a reservoir of any of the capacities given, however, this objection is in a measure overcome, as it seldom happens that there are more than three or four days without wind and the supply in the tank will usually tide over these periods. A ten-foot windmill, with pump and tower, and five thousand gallon tank and tower for same complete, will cost about three hundred dollars. This outfit ought, under all ordinary conditions, to serve for from ten to fifteen thousand plants.

As already mentioned, windmills have the objection of being uncertain in action. They furthermore do not give the facilities for spraying that can be obtained with other power. To obtain twenty pounds pressure, it will be necessary to have the tank raised more than forty feet above the beds, and this is not always practicable. Our preference is therefore for an economical power that is ready at short notice and at all times and can be used for developing pressure as it is needed. Such a machine is to be found in many of the gasoline engines now on the market and which can be bought at very reasonable figures. A two horse-power engine, complete with pump for either deep or shallow well, can be bought for two hundred to two hundred and fifty dollars. A tank of three thousand gallons capacity will increase the cost fifty dollars, so that the total expense of an outfit of this kind will be no more than a windmill. By using a ten gallon closed steel expansion tank for an air chamber water can be pumped directly into the pipe system at a pressure of twenty-five to thirty or forty pounds per square inch. The system can have a safety valve at some convenient point, with the overflow so arranged as to go into the main storage reservoir. With this plan the water can be drawn from the reservoir for ordinary watering, and for spraying the water can be forced by the engine and pump directly into the pipes. The cost of running such an engine is merely nominal. We have used one for several years and find that one dollar a month for gasoline and lubricating oil will give us five hundred gallons of water a day. A thousand gallons of water a day, which is enough for ten to fifteen thousand plants, would probably not cost more than two dollars or two dollars and fifty cents a month. Such gasoline engines if ignited with an electric spark are perfectly safe, can be started or stopped in a moment, and with ordinary care will last for years.

In piping houses there should be one pipe along each path, with hose connections fifty feet apart. For five houses, each one hundred feet by twelve feet, the main water pipe should be one and one-half inches in diameter, with an inch lateral in each house. The hose connections should be three-quarters of an inch, as it does not pay to use one inch hose. It rarely happens that watering goes on in more than one house at a time, so that the one and one-half inch main will be found large enough.

We do not believe there is any special advantage in heating the water in winter. In fact so far as our experience goes cold water is just as good as warm water. This is the general conclusion where careful comparative experiments have been made. It is sometimes an advantage to be able to use liquid fertilizers, and for this purpose a small tank of five hundred to eight hundred gallons should be provided. It should have a separate pipe system, one-inch pipe being large enough all round. If this tank can be set in a barn loft or some slightly elevated place where its contents will not freeze it will be an advantage. The additional cost of a tank of this kind, with pipes and fittings, will be about seventy-five dollars. Such a tank would have sufficient capacity for furnishing liquid food for eight to ten thousand plants.

CHAPTER V.

PROPAGATING, SELECTING, PLANTING, CLEANING, WATERING, ETC.

PROPAGATING.

The violet may be propagated in a number of ways, and as much of the success in growing the crop depends on proper methods we shall go into some detail as to the various practices followed.

One of the most common methods is to divide the crown. This can be done whenever there is sufficient crown to divide, but the common way is to make the divisions in spring after the flowering season is over. The plant is merely lifted with a spade or trowel, and after all the dirt is shaken off the roots the plant is pulled apart or cut apart, as one may think proper. In dividing such a crown young plants of various kinds will be found. Some will have long, "leggy" stems, with many leaf scars upon them; some will be short and stocky; some will have hard, woody roots, while others will show white, clean-growing roots covered with young feeding rootlets and root hairs. It is the general practice to throw away the scrawny plants and to put the others in soil or sand, or in a mixture of both, in order to induce further root development and growth. Some make a practice of putting the young plants in a frame outside, setting them in rows about three inches apart and two inches distant in the row. If

31.—*Cuttings with hard, wiry roots, from divided crowns.*

sand is used about four inches is spread on the ground, and after being firmed with a brick or board the young plants are set in with a dibble. Whitewashed sash is kept over the frame and

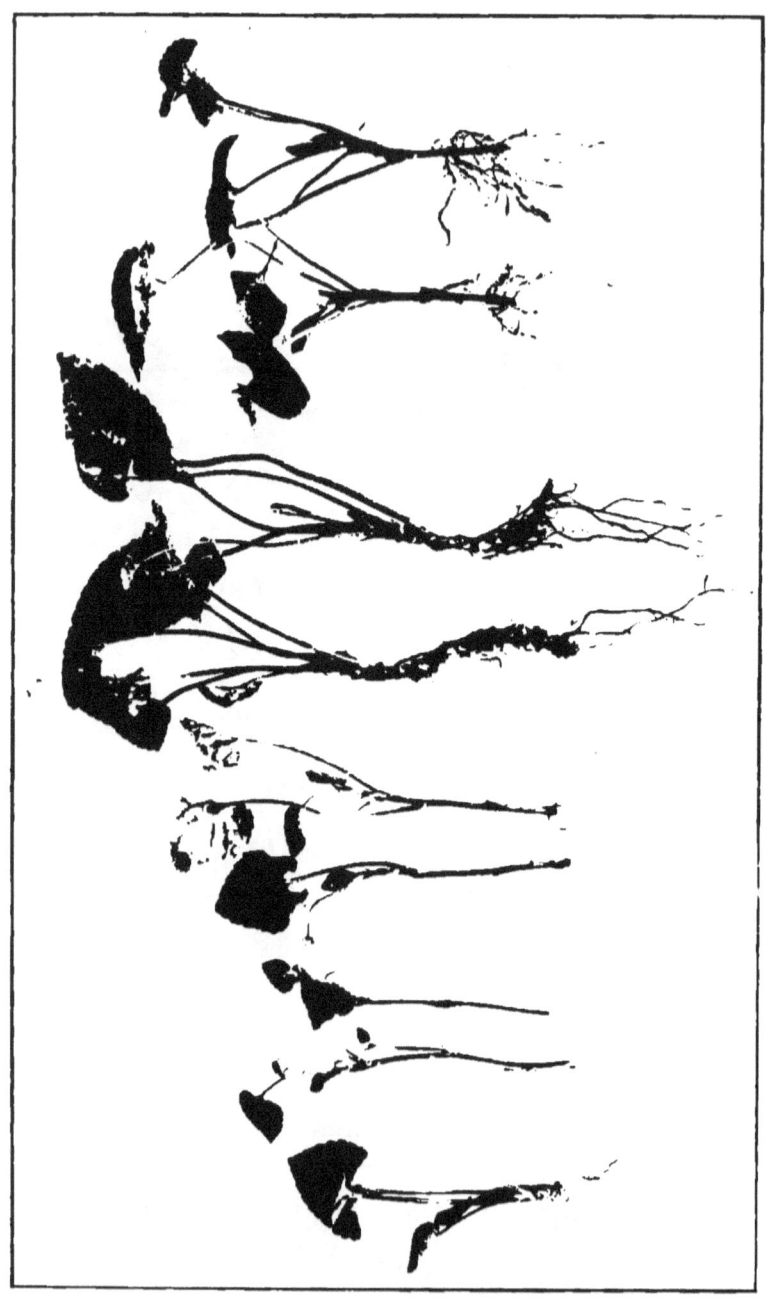

32.—*Various kinds of cuttings from a divided crown. The two cuttings on the right are the only ones worth planting; the two large ones are too old and woody.*

plenty of air is given night and day when the weather permits. As the plants are never put out in this way until the first or middle of April no heat is required. In case soil is used care is taken to add about three inches of good rotten manure to ordinary garden soil. The manure is thoroughly worked in and the ground is made as fine as it is possible to make it with rake and spade. It should never be packed. When smoothed off set the plants the same as described for sand. In both cases the plants must be watched carefully and syringed every bright day in order to keep down red spider, taking care not to over-wet the soil. In six or eight weeks after setting in frames as described, the plants will be ready to transplant to the place where they are to make their summer growth.

There are many objections to propagating plants in this way and the best growers have long since abandoned it. In dividing the crown, and thereby carrying over each year some of the old roots, various diseases affecting the former are carried over also, and if the practice is continued from year to year the tendency is to gradually develop a weak, non-resistant stock. The grower in such cases gradually finds himself losing his ability to get good plants and usually satisfies his conscience by saying that luck is against him. We have examined thousands of apparently strong, vigorous plants, after being lifted in the spring

33.—*Common form of cutting from divided crown. This will make a good plant if properly rooted in soil.*

preparatory to division, but have never yet found one where the roots, both young and old, did not show disease. Of these diseases we shall speak in the proper place; suffice it to say here that they are of such a nature that they gradually continue their insidious work after the young plant is put out, and while the latter may appear strong when it is put in the ground, the trouble is present, and after a while, when an extra strain comes, the effects, in one form or another, will surely appear.

Another serious objection to this method is that it must necessarily be done late, after blooming time is over or nearly over. This in many sections will delay the work of propagation to such an extent that if unusual weather conditions prevail through April or May much injury will result to the young plants. If a hot spell of weather comes on, as it often does in the early part of May, the young plants are sure to suffer, and weak, stunted stock is the result. We have never found it safe to put in stock after April fifteenth.

Another method of propagation, and one open to fewer objections than the last, consists in cutting the offshoots, or cuttings, from the main plant any time from the first of February to the middle of March. In this case the main plant is not disturbed, but the young offshoots, which in good plants are found in abundance, are cut off, only those being selected which show young, white roots. These roots in most cases have never reached the soil, but are sent out into the semi-dark, moist air, made so by the plant as a whole. A good, strong crown will give from ten to twenty cuttings, such as we have described, between the first part of February and the middle of March. As soon as the cuttings are removed they should be thrown into a box with a lid or cover, so as to

34.—*Lath box, or flat, for rooted cuttings.*

keep them from wilting. When a sufficient quantity has been cut they are trimmed up and placed in soil as follows:

Prepare the soil several weeks in advance, using four parts good rotten sod and one part finely rotted manure. Mix thoroughly and screen through an ordinary sand screen or anything having a similar-sized mesh. Keep the soil where it cannot get too wet and never handle it when there is too much moisture present. The soil being prepared, make a lot of boxes, using for the ends strips of undressed white pine one inch thick, three inches wide, and fourteen inches long. For the sides and bottom use ordinary laths cut exactly in half. In making the boxes put on the bottom first, nailing on the two outside laths at the start, then filling in between with others, allowing about a quarter of an inch space between each two pieces of lath. The bottom being made, put on the sides. Each side will take two pieces of lath without space between them. The boxes are now ready to fill with soil, but before doing this spread on the bottom of each box a thin coating of wet sphagnum moss to keep the soil from washing out. Put in enough soil to stand about half an inch higher than the edges of the box, then take a brick and gently press the soil down so that it is uniformly about half an inch below the edges of the box. Set the cuttings with a dibble, so that they will average one hundred to the box.

In one box put thirteen rows of eight plants each, in another twelve rows of eight plants each, and so on. After setting out in this way, the plants are shaded and watered carefully for a few days, and then moved outside into a cold frame or preferably kept in a house where they can be looked after at all times. If put outside they should be kept covered with a whitewashed sash. Where sashes are at hand we prefer to make a temporary house out of them. Such a house has already been described and it will be found that the plants can be looked after much better in them than in a frame. Moreover they will grow better because the air can be kept more moist, diseases and insects can be kept down, and all conditions necessary for growth can be managed to better advantage.

We mention the ordinary cold frame with sash not because we favor it, but merely to show that they have been given fair trial and have been found wanting. This method of propagation applies particularly to the Campbell violet. If all the conditions are carefully watched, fine plants can be grown in this way. We do not advise using boxes or flats with close bottoms as drainage is not so good and the roots in consequence will not develop so well. Roots need air at all times, and where this is given through proper soil, proper drainage, and proper watering, it is astonishing the way the young plants start off and grow.

The third method of propagation and the one generally followed by growers of Marie Louise, consists in taking cuttings from the crowns any time between the middle of January and the middle of March. These cuttings in many cases have already made some air roots, but these should all be trimmed off at the same time the cutting proper is trimmed up. After trimming, the cuttings are put in sand to root. The sand is an important item. It should be moderately coarse and very clean, especially as regards decaying leaves or organic matter of any kind. If obtained from creeks or small streams it is apt to have too much organic matter in it. River sand and bank sand are the best. At Poughkeepsie most of the propagating sand is obtained from banks which crop out at various places, and it is almost wholly free from organic matter. The banks are really veins or strata of sand deposited ages ago. One cannot be too particular about the sand, and while we cannot describe exactly the kind to use, the few hints thrown out will enable the man of intelligence to properly exercise his judgment. We make it a point never to use the sand but once, as it is cheaper to get new sand than to have the cuttings infected with disease.

The sand may be put in boxes as already described for soil. It should be pressed a little more firmly than the soil and watered before putting in the cuttings. The cuttings we put in with a dibble the size of a lead pencil, two hundred cuttings to a box. After filling the boxes the cuttings should be looked after carefully for about two weeks or more. During very bright days they should be covered with single sheets of newspaper, and if the weather is warm and the sun bright the papers should have a dash of water thrown on them with the sprinkling can during the heat of the day. Place the cuttings in a sash

102 CARE OF PLANTS.

35.—*Sand-rooted cuttings, ready to plant in flats filled with soil.*

house as already described, or if there is room in the houses proper keep them there. Never allow them, under any circumstances, to wilt, for if they do it means another reduction in the total output of salable flowers. Where facilities are at hand the cuttings can be rooted in a cutting bench, using about three inches of sand firmed and watered. Put the cuttings in rows about one and one-half inches apart in the row. The cutting bench must be carefully shaded and must be so arranged that currents of air cannot sweep over it. The shed house, with glass roof sloping to the north, already described, forms an excellent place for such a bench. It requires four to eight weeks for cuttings put in sand as described to root properly. They may stay in longer than this without injury, but as soon as they are well rooted they should be transferred to lath boxes containing soil, one hundred to a box. If there is space in the greenhouse the rooted cuttings may be set in one of the beds. Set in rows two inches apart and one inch in the row, using a dibble made by trimming to a point a piece of broom handle six or eight inches long. Never use old soil for these cuttings, that is, soil that has once been used for violets. It costs very little extra labor to get fresh soil for the purpose and the labor will pay a hundred fold.

The principal object of this transplanting is to get good, strong, clean roots. We have had

36.—*Sand-rooted cuttings, ideal type, ready to put in soil.*

excellent success in this matter by throwing the old soil out of a bed to a depth of eight inches and then putting in about two inches of coarse coal ashes, broken clinkers, and the like. On top of this put two inches of sifted coal ashes, and finally four inches of good soil, made, mixed, and sifted as already described. The roots run down into the ashes and come out clean, white, and beautiful, and covered with root hairs.

Growers attempt, once in a while, to set directly from the sand to the beds where the plants are to make their growth. We have tried this plan, but cannot recommend it, as the risk in handling the plants is too great. If cloudy, damp weather follows after the planting no harm may result, but if it should be bright and warm the plants will suffer in spite of all that can be done. There are other objections to this plan, but they need not be mentioned here, as the best growers do not follow the practice at all.

We have now described the three principal methods followed in propagation. The last we recommend to those who have had considerable experience and who are growing Marie Louise. Our preference is for a combination of the second and third methods. In both cases the cuttings are taken from the plants as they stand in the bed. Those which have good, clean, white roots can be put in the soil as already described, but those which are just as good in every way except as to the number of roots, may have all the latter cut off and made to make new ones in the sand. Following this practice, about half the cuttings go into the soil and half into sand. This practice is especially commendable where Campbells are grown, but for Marie Louise, as already pointed out, the sand method throughout is believed to be the best.

The plants when placed in soil as already described are to stand there until they are finally set in the beds, which south of New York, Pittsburg, and Chicago should not be later than the first of June. North of this they may run till the middle of June, or at the very latest the first of July. Leaving out the first practice entirely, it will be seen that in the second the young plants stand in soil-filled flats or boxes from sixty to one hundred and twenty days and then are set directly where they are to grow for flowering. In the third practice the young plants are in sand about fifty days, when they are transferred to soil where they remain until planting time, which runs, according to locality, from the first of June to the first of July. Any one by managing properly and having not over twenty thousand plants ought to be able to do all his planting in fifteen to twenty days. In our section, Washington, we prefer to plant between the first of May and the first of June.

We have omitted the practice of fall propagation, but it will be well to discuss it briefly as some of the older growers believed in it on the ground that it was the only way the stock could be maintained in a healthy condition. Their argument was that the violet is a plant that needs a period of rest, and that propagating in spring just after the plant had been pushed through winter flowering is contrary to nature's methods of increasing the plants. It is true that the violet makes its principal effort in the way of sending out runners in the fall, and theoretically this would be the proper time to propagate, as good wood can then be had in abundance. Practically, however, there are many objections to the plan. Adopting it necessitates carrying the young plants through the winter, and, no matter how much care is exercised in watching them, they nearly always suffer either from being kept too cold or too warm, too dry or too moist. In other words, despite every precaution they get stunted or checked so severely that many of them never rally from the shock, consequently do not prove as vigorous as cuttings made in the spring and properly handled.

Another question to consider, and one that we have found of much importance, is that during their long stand in flats or beds they are apt to become infected with one or more of the several stem and root diseases, and while these may not be plainly evident in the spring, they are present, nevertheless, and will develop and do serious injury later. There is this to be said, however, that choosing between the methods of division after blooming time and propagating in the fall, we would prefer the latter, because we believe that better results will follow. Finally, in using the fall-rooted plants there is always the danger of the plants getting too big. It is as bad to have a plant too big as it is to have it too small, and if set too early or started too early the growth will become so heavy in hot weather that it will be found impossible to keep down diseases and insects. If a grower has everything at his disposal in the way of houses and facilities for handling the young plants it would probably be well to propagate some of the stock in the fall, but if he has to put up with the ordinary facilities he had better leave fall cuttings alone. Fall propagating really means a special house for the proper care and handling of the young plants through a period of six or eight months—a handling so that they will not grow too much or too little (problems that are beyond the reach of most men). We have now described the mere act of propagating or increasing the number of plants and have next to consider the most important question connected with violet growing, namely, the selection of stock with a view of increasing vigor and productiveness.

SELECTION OF STOCK FOR VIGOR AND PRODUCTIVENESS.

To grasp this question fully we must first realize that the violet, like other plants, is a plastic organism—that within a certain range it has power to change or to adapt itself to the conditions which surround it. This plasticity or adaptability of the plant is of the utmost importance, for if all its functions were fixed absolutely it could not suffer any change for long, however slight. We find, therefore, in practice, that plants grown in one section and moved to another behave differently— it may be in the matter of time of blooming, quantity of flowers, character of foliage, size or color of flowers, length of flower stem, or in many other directions. Recognizing this fact, and those that are naturally correlated with it, we have the important practical conclusion that the only way for a man to attain the maximum results from the plants is to work steadily, intelligently, and rationally toward the end of developing a strain which will fit the conditions which practice and judgment enable him to provide. Of course, the man himself is limited in this matter, but he should endeavor first of all to find out what his limitations are and then concentrate his efforts in the field where there is hope of practical results. As a matter of fact, the limitations are more fancied than real and where

37.—Pedigree plant, with tag showing dates of picking and yield of flowers.

the work is intelligently undertaken and carried out it is astonishing what power is put within the grasp.

It is seldom that violet growers average more than fifty flowers to the plant for the season. There is no good reason why this number should not be increased to one hundred or even one hundred and fifty flowers per plant without additional room, additional heat, additional fertilizers, or additional work of any kind except in the care necessary to keep up the stock by proper selection. How then should this selection be started, and how should it be continued in order to reap the full benefit from it? To start at the beginning, it will be found that the first stock of plants, no matter where obtained, will show differences: Some will be small, some large; some will give long-stemmed flowers, others flowers with short stems; some will show a tendency to throw flowers off in color; some will have a straggling habit of growth, others will be compact, with large leaves on long petioles. As the season for flower picking arrives these plants should be carefully gone over and the grower should fix in his own mind his ideal or type. It does not take long to learn what plants more closely approximate the type. Out of one thousand plants there may not the first year be more than a hundred that show the characteristics he is after. We cannot put down in black and white what these characteristics

112 CARE OF PLANTS.

38.—Bed of pedigree plants.

are, except in the most general way. The plants should be vigorous and give every evidence that they are growing. They should have a compact, symmetrical appearance. The leaves should be glossy, green, large, and on long petioles, and should feel, when you run your hand over them, like living, growing things, and not like they were made of leather or cloth. If a hundred or less of such plants are found stake them before flowering commences, and to each stake tie an ordinary shipping tag. Push the stake well into the soil so that it will not interfere with working the beds, and tie the tag on securely so that it will not come off or get lost. Each plant is then given a number, which is never duplicated. We give one hundred plants as the limit for the first year's work, for this is about as many as one can well handle until more experience is gained. There would, therefore, be one hundred numbers—from one to one hundred. Every time a tagged plant is reached while picking, count the number of flowers and put down on the tag the date and number of flowers picked. We presume there will be some who upon reading this, will say: "I have not the time to do this and what is the good of it all anyway?" These are the men who insist that luck governs the question, and while they will always be found they are constantly vexed with ups and downs and sooner or later quit. As a matter of fact, it takes very little time to do what has been outlined and anyone who will follow the practice for three years will be willing to hire additional help, if necessary, to keep up the work, because he will see that it pays.

When the season's work is over it will be found that the tagged plants show many interesting facts. They show the total number of flowers picked and the number picked each month, and they show too the relation of flower yield to weather conditions if one wishes to carry the matter into this field. Some plants have grown fifty flowers, others as many as one hundred and fifty. Some will give the greatest number of flowers in December and January, others in February and March. Here then, are practical points that should at once be taken advantage of. Vigor, health, compactness of growth being equal, we would want our plants to yield an many flowers as possible, and at a time when they are worth the most money; so that of two plants both of which give a hundred flowers, we would give the preference to the one that yields the most flowers during December and January rather than to the one that gives the greater yield during February and March. Of the pedigree stock we would eliminate all plants where the yield the first year dropped below seventy-five flowers. The second year we would eliminate all plants that failed to give more than ninety flowers, and the third year all those that failed to give a hundred good blooms.

Each plant can be counted on to give not less than ten first-class cuttings, so that if only fifty plants come up to the standard the first year they will give at least five hundred good rooted cuttings for the second season. Each of these plants should carry the number of their parent, with an additional mark to indicate the season; for example, the ten plants from number one the first year would all be recorded as plants a, next year the plants from these would be plants b, and so on. If the work is carried out well the first year, three hundred plants, representing the best of the five hundred, can be staked the second season. These receive their specified numbers, are watched as before, and will give from one thousand to one thousand five hundred good plants for the next season's crop. Working in this way, and of course keeping clearly before one the importance of looking after every detail of culture, the average yield can be brought up to the one hundred mark, where it may be kept as long as the proper vigilance and intelligence are exercised in the work. We are satisfied that two-thirds of the failures in growing violets come about from not fully recognizing the principles we have here set forth. Left to itself, or if not properly assisted, the tendency of the violet is to retrograde, partly no doubt because it has been grown so long under abnormal conditions and partly for other reasons, which it is not necessary to discuss in detail here. We find in it very much the condition of a loaded car on a steep grade. It is always ready to go down hill the moment we take off the brake or remove the block from the rail. The further it goes the more difficult it is to stop, and if we do not put forth some effort there will be a general smash-up sooner or later. On the other hand, by dint of much labor we can slowly push up grade, but we are always confronted with the fact that the moment we lose our watchfulness the down-hill motion commences, and away goes everything we have gained.

The author's work is done when he points out the facts and principles involved, and it remains for the reader to do the rest.

PLANTING.

We have pointed out in the previous chapter how to prepare the soil and have shown in the first part of this chapter how the plants are to be cared for until the time for planting. As already stated, we prefer to get our plants out permanently between the first of May and the first of June in latitudes south of New York, but north of this planting may be delayed fifteen or twenty days. Having the soil stacked and ready near the houses the first operation is to throw out the old plants and remove six inches of the soil from the beds. The old plants are merely lifted with a spade, the earth is shaken off, and then they are thrown outside into a heap to be hauled away to the dump or burned. If hauled away we want to get them as far away from the houses as possible. In any event they should never be allowed to lie around and rot and decay.

The soil is best handled in wheelbarrows. It is hauled out and thrown in a heap close by, to be finally disposed of when more time is at hand. When the six inches of soil is taken out all boards are examined and if any are found rotted they are taken out and new ones put in. The beds are next spaded up with a fork and air-slacked lime is thrown over the ground in sufficient quantity to thoroughly whiten it. The new soil is then brought in with the wheelbarrows and dumped into the beds. Enough soil is brought in to fill the beds just even with the boards. In no case is the soil rolled, walked on, or packed in any way. When sufficient soil is in the bed the latter is leveled off with a rake, all clods, stones, large sticks, etc., being thrown out. Finally the beds are made smooth and level by means of a straight-edged board four inches wide and not longer than the width of the bed.

The bed is now ready to be marked off. This can be done in a number of ways, the main object being to get the plants set as nearly in straight rows as possible, eight by nine inches apart. It often happens that the board marking the walk is not straight and if the plants are set straight by a line they appear crooked on account of the board, as that is what the eye usually follows. To keep the rows straight with the board use a simple T square made of a piece of four inch white pine. By using the board of the walk as a base for the square all the rows come in line with the walk, and at least appear more pleasing to the eye even if they are not mathematically straight. By means of a saw permanent lines are marked off nine inches apart on the board forming the edge of the walk. Similar lines are made eight inches apart on the square. The square can then be moved rapidly along over the ground and a hole made with a dibble where the plant is to be set. We usually try to have the plants set back at least five inches from the edge of the walk, so it takes a little figuring at first to tell how to divide the space across the bed. As soon as the bed is marked the plants are set, as better results are obtained in this way than where the ground is allowed to settle. In case it is not practicable to plant at once and if the ground settles too much before planting can be done, the beds should be freshly turned up with a fork and then raked down and smoothed as before described.

The plants are cut out of the boxes or bed where they have been growing and all dead leaves and buds are trimmed off. They are then carried to the bed where they are to be planted and laid opposite each mark made by the dibble. The advantage of having the stock plants in light flats comes in here, for the flats can be carried to the bed and the plants cut out there—we say cut out, for we usually use a putty knife for the purpose. This is first run down between the rows of plants in the box, after which a cut is made between each two plants. In this way each plant comes out with a square piece of soil and the roots are disturbed very little. One good man can set as fast as two or three can prepare the plants as described. Where the reach is less than five feet the plants can be set from the walk, but if the beds are so wide that one cannot reach, planting is done from a board laid across the bed, but not so that it will compact the soil. Use a board twelve inches wide and work backwards in planting. Adopting this plan two rows can be planted without moving the board. The planting itself is an important item, and many plants will be lost and others injured unless care is exercised. The grower himself had better attend to this matter. We have never found anything better than the fingers for planting. A slight hole is made and the square of earth containing the young plant and its roots is pushed into the loose soil. A movement of the hand around the plant levels the soil and firms it and the work is done. Having the beds filled and leveled and the plants furnished, one man can mark the soil and set three hundred

120　CARE OF PLANTS.

39.—*Violet culture under lath sheds in California (N. B. Pierce, Santa Ana, Cal., photographer).*

plants an hour. If the day is warm and bright it will be necessary to water the plants as they are put out. One can plant for an hour, however, and then water, allowing the water to run gently from the end of the hose, and following the rows so as not to plow up the ground. At this season of the year it is of course necessary to have all ventilators and doors open in order to get plenty of air. The glass also should be well shaded with whitewash or with white lead mixed with turpentine, either one to be put on with a brush. We have used laths for shading, but abandoned them for the reason that they interfere with the light in such a way as to hinder growth. The shading should be only moderately heavy, but it should be kept as nearly as possible the same throughout the entire year, that is, winter and summer we have found it an advantage to shade, but this may not hold good further north where sunshine is less abundant.

All of our directions, it will be seen, apply to plants grown under glass throughout the year. We do not recommend field planting of violets anywhere, that is, if it is intended to grow them for flowering in houses the following winter. It is very important, however, to have some reserve plants, for there is always more or less loss in the beds. Here again the cheap frame house comes into good use, for it is well adapted for growing reserve plants. It is best to count on a loss of ten

122 CARE OF PLANTS.

40.—*Field culture of violets in Virginia. Frames are put on in September.*

per cent, although this is heavier than it ought to be. For ten thousand plants, therefore, it would be necessary to have a reserve of at least one thousand plants to draw upon.

When frames alone are used the plants can be set in two ways: First, the frames themselves can be put down where they are to stay and the plants set in rows eight by nine inches, as already described; second, the frames can be made, as already described, in sixteen foot lengths and stored until wanted. The plants are then set directly in the open, nine inches apart in the row, the rows being just long enough so that the frame will fit over them. There are so many objections to these methods and the obstacles to overcome are so great that we do not recommend them except in violet farming. Shade here is of the greatest importance during the summer and where the plants are grown in open frames or without frames this can only be brought about by using lath screens or something similar. The screens when made should not be too dense and should be raised at least four feet above the plants. In southern California violets are grown the whole season with no other protection than screens, made of laths, raised about eight feet above the plants. The flowers are shipped to Los Angeles and other points and are of fair quality.

After the planting is completed and everything about the place has been cleaned up and put in shape, the serious work of caring for the plants commences.

CLEANING, WATERING, SYRINGING, MULCHING, AND FEEDING.

Eternal vigilance is necessary in the matter of cleaning. We try to get over the plants at least once a week, cutting off all yellow and dying leaves and gently stirring the surface of the soil with the fingers. All weeds, too, are pulled up or torn up in the stirring. In cleaning we never use anything but a knife, as pulling the leaves off is a bad practice for it is apt to tear the bark and open the way for the attacks of fungi. Toward the middle of August the runners will begin to come, and they must be cut off as soon as possible. Many abortive flowers will appear too and they must not be allowed to stay on the plant. In cleaning we have made it an invariable practice to throw all dead leaves, runners, etc., into a box or basket, emptying these into a barrel or box outside at suitable intervals. We do not believe it wise to throw the material into the walks, for no matter how soon the latter may be swept, some of the decaying material is trampled upon and in this way the first steps toward the beginning of disease may be taken. The only safe rule to follow is to never allow a leaf of any kind to lie around and decay in the houses or frames. We have time and time again seen growers cleaning their plants, especially where they are in frames, and throwing the dead leaves, runners, and weeds out under their feet, to be trampled into the mud. Such growers have fair success for a season or two, then wonder why it is that diseases and insect pests steadily increase until they finally get the upper hand. Cleanliness at all times and a thorough destruction of all diseased leaves, cuttings, and plants are matters that should never be neglected.

Watering to the ordinary man may really seem like a simple matter, but it is one of the most important factors in the growth of this or any other crop. No hard and fast rules can be laid down on this subject. Water when the plants need it, which can only be determined by experience. We never water over head, but use the end of a three-quarter inch hose held in such a way that the water runs out freely but not forcibly. If the water comes out with too much force the soil is puddled and the plants may be washed up. When the plants are still young and the ground is soft a good plan is to fasten to the end of the hose an ordinary tin pancake turner, such as can be bought anywhere for ten cents. This can be fastened to the hose by a rubber band and will spread the water so that it will fall in a thin sheet about four inches wide. The water soaks in when put on in this way and seldom causes the formation of a crust—the thing to be avoided.

Plants in hot weather require water almost every day. At no time should the plants be allowed to become dry, nor should water be given so often that the soil is kept constantly in a pasty condition.

In our judgment the best results will be obtained when the variation of the moisture in the soil is allowed the widest range the plants will stand. What this is cannot be given in words as too many conditions are involved. It is a question that must be studied by each individual and by him worked out for his own case. The point we wish to make is that better growth can be obtained by allowing a certain range or variation in the moisture content of the soil than where an attempt is made to keep the moisture content at one point or near one point. If, for example, we find that in a certain type of soil the best growth is obtained where the maximum moisture content approximates twenty per cent, it will be best not to attempt to hold the moisture steadily at this point, but rather to allow a variation of five to eight per cent, as this is more apt to give optimum conditions for growth than where an effort is put forth to hold it at one point.

It is not necessary here to go into a discussion of the physiological questions involved in this matter. Suffice it to say that we may look at the plant in the light of a machine kept in operation in part by stimuli from without. Stimuli may come by changes in conditions and if everything works in harmony perfect growth is the result.

As the season advances the plants will require more and more water, and every precaution will have to be taken not to let them wilt or to get on the dry side so often as to check growth. The plants must be kept growing without a check of any kind, so that by the middle of September they practically cover the ground.

From the time of planting constant care must be exercised in the matter of syringing. Plants ought to be syringed throughout the summer and early fall not less than three times a week. We will discuss this question more fully in the chapter on insects and diseases as the syringing is mainly to keep down red spider. Always select bright days for the syringing so as to have the plants dry off before night. As the season advances and the plants grow larger much care must be exercised in syringing, otherwise serious results may follow, as will be pointed out further on. By the first or middle of October it will be necessary to withhold all water from the foliage, and if the spraying has been thorough this can be done without fear of injury from spider.

About the middle of August we like to give the beds a thin mulching of finely rotted manure. Horse manure is best for this purpose, as it works up fine and dries out better on the bed. Put on just enough to cover the ground and work it well around the plants. The manure mulching serves to keep the ground moist and free from weeds. It also keeps the flowers cleaner when they come and checks the growth of slime and green molds that sometimes appear on the soil. Mulching with sphagnum and with pine shavings has been tried, but both were abandoned in favor of the rotted horse manure.

Feeding after the plants are once established is an important matter, but our advice to the beginners is to let it severely alone. There are three or four don'ts that come in aptly at this point: (1) Don't imagine that you must feed your plants in order to get the best results. This is true of some crops, but not of the violet. (2) Don't trifle with chemicals. They may be all right in the hands of an expert, but it is like putting strong medicine into the hands of a layman and turning him loose to doctor his friends. (3) If you must use chemical fertilizers don't experiment on all your plants, but set aside a few dozen in one bed and a few dozen in another, make your trials carefully, and compare the results obtained with those where no chemicals have been used. We know from many experiments that the only safe way is to feed as little as possible, as the plants if let alone will take care of themselves provided the soil is prepared as we have described elsewhere. When you do feed apply only manure water made by soaking good, strong cow manure in water, using about one-half bushel of manure to the barrel of water. A watering with this kind of fertilizer every ten or fifteen days during the winter will do no harm and may do good. Great care, however, must be exercised in keeping the manure water fresh and odorless. If it is allowed to sour and become offensive it should never be run on the beds as the flowers will take up the odor. If we were growing roses, carnations, or chrysanthemums our discussion of the use of liquid fertilizers would be different, as these are crops that can stand feeding while the violet cannot—at least this has been our experience and the result of observations in many places and under widely varying conditions.

In concluding this chapter there are several points to which we wish to call special attention: (1) Never delay propagating the plants until late in spring for such stock cannot be depended upon. (2) Always propagate two or even three times more plants than your houses or frames will hold in order to cover risks and to have plenty of stock for selection. (3) From the time the cutting leaves the parent plant until it has fulfilled its mission as a full grown crown, never allow it to become checked in any way. (4) Adopt a rigid system of selection. (5) Practice cleanliness about every part of the work. (6) Apply water with due regard for the plants' wants and not by any set of rules.

CHAPTER VI.

TEMPERATURE CONDITIONS AND VENTILATION.

The violet must be kept cool and any attempt to force it by heat will prove disastrous. For Campbell violets an effort should be made to keep the night temperature between forty-five and fifty degrees, with a day temperature, in bright weather, ten to fifteen degrees higher. Marie Louise should be kept cooler, say forty to forty-five at night, with day temperature fifty-five to sixty.

When the weather is cloudy and cold do not attempt to keep the inside temperature in the sixties or even the fifties. Probably the safest rule to follow with the violet at all times is to manage the conditions so as to have, as near as possible, an average temperature of eight or ten degrees above freezing. For example, if the temperature outside is thirty degrees above zero in the day time and the weather cloudy, keep the temperature of the houses not more than forty to forty-five degrees. If sunny weather prevails the temperature will naturally go higher, but do not allow it to get above sixty degrees, if it can be avoided by ventilation and allowing the heating pipes to become cold. In the climate of Washington and vicinity it is very seldom necessary to have any fire in the heater during sunny weather, unless the temperature outside is excessively cold and high winds are blowing. As a rule the heat of the sun will be amply sufficient to keep the houses in good condition, so that it is always safest to either bank or cover the fires, or else allow them to die out entirely during the day. Of course, farther north these rules will not apply, but in a general way they will hold good everywhere. It must be understood that the violet is unlike the rose or carnation as regards heat, and as already pointed out any attempt to force it will result in overgrowth of leaves· and blasting of the flowers.

Ventilation has already been briefly mentioned, but it is important to call attention to this matter more specifically, for it is of the highest importance to realize the necessity of giving plenty of air to the plant at all times. It is impossible to give directions as to how and when to ventilate. The violet is a lover of fresh air and plenty of it, so that there is seldom a day when more or less air should not be given. It must not be supposed that this is a simple matter, and one that can be left to the hired man or some irresponsible person. No two days in the year are exactly alike, so far as the requirements for ventilation are concerned. It frequently happens that air will be needed the first thing in the morning, and it should be given, not all at once, but little by little as the day advances and the plants require it. In the course of such a day changes may come about, necessitating letting the air off, so that there is a constant changing either one way or another throughout the entire day. Even at night it is necessary to observe these precautions in order to keep the plants in good condition. It has been our practice to allow the houses to run just as cold as possible in the early part of February and later. It will not injure the plants late in the season to occasionally allow a little frost to get in. This will hold back the flowers and will give more returns as the season advances. In March or April, if the weather is mild, the doors and ventilators should be open at all times in order to get plenty of fresh air. If this practice is not followed the growth will be so rapid that blossoming will soon cease and there will be no flowers for Easter.

One of the chief reasons why it is difficult for a grower to handle violets in connection with other crops is the failure to furnish proper temperature and ventilation for the violets. The tendency in such cases is always to give too much heat, and this more than anything else will soon manifest itself in the appearance of small, poorly colored flowers.

The same care given in the houses must be observed where frames are used. Plants in a frame will burn up on a bright day unless air is properly given. Watch the conditions carefully and give air when the plants need it. Often it will only be necessary to raise one frame in five an inch or two in the back. Then again it may be necessary to raise all three or four inches to keep the plants from suffering. On mild days in winter it will improve the plants to occasionally take the frames entirely off, allowing the air to dry out the soil and the sun to warm it. Snow must be removed as soon as possible, but it often happens that a good coating of snow will save the plants from freezing. If it promises to be very cold after a snow it is best to leave the latter on for twenty-four or even for forty-eight hours. If left longer than this the plants may suffer for want of light.

It may be of interest to give in tabulated form the temperature records of a violet house for five months of the winter period. These records, which were made for the writer by Mr. Geo. Saltford, of Poughkeepsie, New York, show the highest, lowest, and average temperatures recorded during the day and also during the night in his houses. A study of the records will be of value to those who desire to keep their houses in the proper condition so far as temperature is concerned. Although made at Poughkeepsie, the records are applicable to most sections where violets are grown.

Record of Night and Day Temperatures and Sunshine for five months.

DECEMBER, 1895.

Date. Dec., 1895.	Night temperature. Degrees F. Readings at 7 A.M.			Day temperature. Degrees F. Readings at 7 P.M.			Sunshine. (10 equals sunshine all day, 8 equals 8-10 of day, etc.)
	Max.	Min.	Mean.	Max.	Min.	Mean.	
13	46	35	40	68	54	61	8
14	47	42	44	64	39	51	10
15	47	42	44	65	44	54	7
16	48	44	46	64	43	53	10
17	48	41	44	64	44	54	10
18	52	43	42	62	46	54	5
19	53	46	49	68	46	57	10
20	58	46	52	72	52	62	7
21	58	53	55	65	53	59	4
22	60	45	54	66	44	55	9
23	54	48	51	65	50	57	6
24	60	46	53	70	47	58	9
25	54	50	52	59	50	54	7
26	55	49	52	62	52	57	4
27	57	44	50	67	46	56	10
28	47	42	44	60	42	51	10
29	52	44	48	56	43	49	7
30	50	40	45	51	43	47	00
31	60	42	51	55	44	49	10
Average, or mean...	53	44	**48**	63	46	**55**	

TEMPERATURE.

JANUARY, 1896.

Date. Jan., 1896.	Night temperature. Degrees F. Readings at 7 A.M.			Day temperature. Degrees F. Readings at 7 P.M.			Sunshine. (10 equals sunshine all day, 8 equals 8-10 of day, etc.)
	Max.	Min.	Mean.	Max.	Min.	Mean.	
1	45	40	42	58	42	50	10
2	46	40	43	61	44	52	9
3	47	44	45	71	46	58	9
4	46	38	42	60	40	50	10
5	41	34	37	63	33	48	10
6	40	31	35	64	44	54	10
7	45	38	41	49	41	45	00
8	46	38	42	61	38	49	10
9	47	38	42	47	41	44	00
10	44	40	42	61	41	51	8
11	47	40	43	67	47	57	00
12	47	42	44	50	47	48	10
13	47	41	44	58	39	48	10
14	47	39	43	58	39	48	10
15	47	35	41	68	36	52	10
16	46	36	41	61	41	51	10
17	45	38	41	59	47	53	8
18	45	39	42	66	39	52	10
19	48	44	46	55	42	48	00
20	43	40	41	61	40	50	5
21	47	40	43	56	41	48	00
22	47	40	43	63	41	52	5
23	44	41	42	58	41	49	7
24	46	41	43	49	40	44	00
25	47	46	46	49	46	47	00
26	48	45	46	55	45	50	2
27	45	41	43	66	39	52	10
28	45	38	41	56	39	47	10
29	44	36	40	65	36	50	10
30	45	40	42	66	45	55	10
31	45	38	41	66	39	52	9
Average, or mean...	46	39	42	59	41	50	

TEMPERATURE AND VENTILATION.

FEBRUARY, 1896.

Date. Feb., 1896.	Night temperature. Degrees F. Readings at 7 A.M.			Day temperature. Degrees F. Readings at 7 P.M.			Sunshine. (10 equals sunshine all day, 8 equals 8-10 of day, etc.)
	Max.	Min.	Mean.	Max.	Min.	Mean.	
1	45	42	43	55	42	48	00
2	50	40	45	69	45	57	10
3	46	38	42	53	39	46	00
4	45	42	43	52	42	47	00
5.	45	42	43	57	44	50	00
6	49	46	47	56	47	51	00
7	46	42	44	59	45	52	2
8	45	42	43	71	44	57	10
9	46	41	43	44	42	43	00
10	44	38	41	70	41	55	10
11	44	38	41	56	39	47	10
12	42	38	40	65	42	53	10
13	46	42	44	47	42	44	00
14	47	38	42	57	39	48	10
15	47	40	43	56	42	49	10
16	49	38	43	62	38	50	10
17	42	35	38	63	37	50	10
18	42	34	38	67	42	54	10
19	47	39	43	54	39	46	7
20	44	37	40	57	37	47	10
21	44	37	40	62	37	49	10
22	45	39	42	62	42	52	10
23	45	37	41	60	45	52	5
24	46	41	43	63	43	53	10
25	47	39	43	62	40	51	10
26	44	39	41	55	41	48	00
27	44	40	42	65	40	52	10
28	44	40	42	60	41	50	4
29	51	44	47	51	49	50	00
Average, or mean...	46	40	**43**	59	42	**50**	

TEMPERATURE.

MARCH, 1896.

Date. Mar., 1896.	Night temperature. Degrees F. Readings at 7 A.M.			Day temperature. Degrees F. Readings at 7 P.M.			Sunshine. (10 equals sunshine all day, 8 equals 8-10 of day, etc.)
	Max.	Min.	Mean.	Max.	Min.	Mean.	
1	51	47	49	62	44	53	00
2	51	44	47	67	42	54	5
3	43	39	41	62	39	50	7
4	44	38	41	63	36	49	10
5	45	38	41	67	43	55	10
6	44	37	40	71	38	54	10
7	51	44	47	64	44	54	5
8	50	41	45	59	39	49	9
9	45	38	41	64	39	51	5
10	44	39	41	55	40	47	5
11	43	39	41	47	41	44	00
12	44	39	41	51	40	45	4
13	42	36	39	62	38	50	10
14	37	34	35	67	41	54	10
15	48	38	43	61	36	48	5
16	45	39	42	56	41	48	00
17	44	41	42	61	43	52	10
18	43	34	38	60	42	51	10
19	45	38	41	61	41	51	00
20	54	42	48	57	40	48	10
21	42	33	40	60	39	49	10
22	41	37	39	67	41	54	9
23	45	35	40	57	38	48	2
24	44	35	39	64	37	50	10
25	44	38	41	67	40	53	10
26	51	40	45	67	48	57	10
27	47	36	41	58	40	49	10
28	49	39	44	64	42	53	10
29	47	40	43	53	44	48	00
30	47	44	45	67	44	55	5
31	49	44	46	80	47	63	10
Average, or mean...	46	39	42	62	41	51	

TEMPERATURE AND VENTILATION.

APRIL, 1896.

Date. April, 1896.	Night temperature. Degrees F. Readings at 7 A.M.			Day temperature. Degrees F. Readings at 7 P.M.			Sunshine. (10 equals sunshine all day, 8 equals 8-10 of day, etc.)
	Max.	Min.	Mean.	Max.	Min.	Mean.	
1	51	39	45	60	47	53	7
2	47	42	44	54	40	47	1
3	41	35	38	67	38	52	5
4	42	36	39	55	41	48	10
5	49	37	43	69	42	55	10
6	47	46	46	57	41	49	5
7	44	39	41	57	40	48	00
8	43	39	41	65	42	53	10
9	44	37	40	47	45	46	10
10	50	42	46	68	44	56	10
11	50	39	44	70	50	60	8
12	51	49	50	79	51	65	9
13	50	44	47	84	50	67	9
14	60	49	54	85	60	72	10
15	67	58	62	93	65	79	10
16	70	59	64	103	69	86	10
17	69	61	65	85	64	74	9
18	72	64	68	103	72	87	9
19	71	61	66	92	70	81	10
20	74	64	69	94	73	83	10
21	72	63	67	91	70	80	4
22	69	60	64	70	43	56	8
23	47	35	41	80	57	68	10
24	60	41	50	85	59	72	9
25	54	42	48	65	54	59	5
26	55	41	48	67	53	60	10
27	58	42	50	73	58	65	10
28	59	40	49	79	60	69	5
29	64	45	54	85	65	75	9
30	57	43	50	84	58	71	10
Average, or mean...	56	46	51	76	54	65	

Average Temperatures.

	Night.	Day.	
December	48	55	Degrees F.
January	42	50	"
February	42	50	"
March	42	51	"
April	51	65	"

CHAPTER VII.

HANDLING AND MARKETING THE CROP.

It must be borne in mind that to grow good flowers is not the only requirement for success. After the flowers are grown they must be marketed, and to do this successfully is one of the most important matters with which we have to deal. Success in this particular respect is in large measure dependent upon the character and temperament of the man. Some men may be excellent growers and yet so lacking in personality and adaptability that they cannot deal with their customers in a satisfactory manner for any length of time. It is very often the case that such men blame everything but the right thing for their inability to get along and for the trouble they have not only with the dealers that handle their stock, but with the men who work for them as well. There is little hope for such people until they can be brought to a realization of the fact that the difficulty is in themselves and not in the things around them. Learn, therefore, to adapt yourself to the conditions as you find them and things will go much easier than when you attempt to mold all conditions to your way of thinking.

At the outset it is necessary to study the needs of your market and try to meet them as fully as possible. When you start you will doubtless be a stranger—at least you will be regarded as such from a business point of view, for business is not prone to recognize sentiment in any of its dealings. You will therefore have to establish your ability to grow good stock, to grow it regularly, and to be able to put it into the hands of your dealer when he wants it. This cannot be done in one or two years, but at the end of three or four seasons, if the work has been carried on in the right way, your reputation will have a fair start.

It is perfectly feasible for a grower who knows his conditions and handles his plants properly, to tell by the first of October how many flowers he can furnish for the following six months; that is, he ought to know within two or three per cent how many flowers he will have for October, November, December, and each succeeding month through March. Knowing this, he is in a position to deal in a businesslike way with the man or men who handle his flowers, for it is as important for the dealer to know, to a reasonable certainty, what he can depend upon as it is for the grower to know what he can furnish. Much of the complaint which arises about poor prices being received for flowers is not because the flowers are not good,

41.—*Violets bunched for Philadelphia market, some of the flowers projecting from the bunch.*

but it is on account of the spasmodic way in which they are sent in and the fact that they have to take their chances with a great mass of stock of this kind. From the last purchaser or consumer to the grower there is a direct connection in this matter. Even though flowers are a luxury, customers soon learn where the supply is steady and the quality high. They recognize this and are willing to pay for it. The dealer in time knows the growers he can depend upon and can afford to pay them a higher price for their stock than the men who can give no reliable assurance as to what they can furnish from one week to another. It is this very fact that emphasizes the importance of growing the plants in houses, for if they are in frames a snow storm or cold snap may close up everything for a week or more, and in the meantime the demand in the city has not diminished in the least.

Outside of what has been said, however, there are many details that influence the success of disposing of stock. Every market has its peculiarities and these must be studied and pandered to. We cannot point out these conditions for they vary so much and change so often that the matter is one that will have to be taken in hand by the grower himself.

The methods of bunching, arranging of the leaves, and other matters all vary in different sections and we can only describe some of the more important ones here. Before proceeding to

42.—Violets bunched for Washington market, using Princess of Wales leaves.

do this, however, it would be well to consider more in detail some of the methods of disposing of the flowers. The grower may sell his flowers direct to the retailer, or he may dispose of them through the commission merchant. Each plan has its advantages and disadvantages and these we shall now point out. No one questions the fact that there are plenty of honest, straightforward business men in both lines. There are frauds of course, but we meet them everywhere, and as soon as one is found out he should be dropped. The retailer pays for the flowers outright and unless the grower is in position to demand something better he will get just half the retail price for his stock; that is, if violets are selling at two dollars per bunch of fifty flowers the grower will get one dollar, if they are selling for one dollar he will get fifty cents. This seems like a big margin of profit for the retailer, but in reality the risks are so many that it is about all he can afford to pay to the grower who cannot count on what he can furnish in the way of quantity or quality. On the other hand, the grower who conducts his business in the proper way can make up his schedule of prices at the beginning of the season, and the retailer, knowing his man and that he can depend upon him, can afford to pay him more. In fact, the prices in such cases should and will run from twenty to twenty-five per cent higher than in the first plan described. On the other hand, the grower who sells to the retailer has no opportunity as a grower to enlarge his reputation, for the purchaser seldom knows who grows the stock. The fact is that a large portion of the purchasers have the innocent delusion that the retailer himself grows all the stock he sells. The grower, therefore, has no way of extending his reputation and if anything should happen to the retailer who handles his flowers, he will have to start over again with a new man, which is a thing not always easy to do. Again, the retailer must necessarily be more exacting in his demands. He has orders to fill at all times of the day and every day in the week, and the grower must always be willing and ready to fill such orders.

In selling through commission merchants the stock is put in competition with others, and its merits will always tell in the hands of a fair merchant—the only kind it pays to deal with. It is true that a commission must be paid, but where this is done and the flowers are put up and delivered properly and in good shape, the net returns will equal those from the retailer. In selling through the commission merchant the grower has practically unlimited opportunity for extending his reputation. Every shipment should indicate plainly who the grower is, and the retailers, who are constantly on the lookout for good material soon learn where they can get it and will pay for it accordingly. Furthermore, the grower in such cases can manage his business so as to pick his flowers at regular times and all of the work about the place can therefore be put on a more systematic basis. Where a grower is so situated that he can reach several good markets within one to eight hours it would be best to combine the two plans, as may frequently be done. The nearest market, which he could reach daily perhaps in person, might be given up to dealing with the retailer, while the commission merchant could be used in the more distant market. It is seldom desirable to sell to more than one retailer in a city, for if you have good stock and your merchant is doing the proper amount of business he can handle without difficulty all you can supply. He will furthermore do it better and more to your advantage than if you attempt to divide up your stock among several retailers. All these matters and many others will have to be studied by each individual, and if done intelligently the best and most profitable methods will soon be learned.

Coming now more particularly to the details of handling the crop, it must be understood that in addition to being put up in an attractive manner the violet to sell at the best price must have other qualities. The stems must be long, and the flowers of a good color, large, and, most important of all, they must be sweet. A violet without sweetness is not wanted anywhere, and a failure to recognize this leads to more trouble than any other one thing connected with the work. Violets properly grown are always sweet, but all the delicious odor may be lost through improper handling. The flower loses its odor rapidly as soon as it is removed from the plant, and the quicker it reaches the retailer's hands the sweeter it will be. Long distance shipments, therefore, are never satisfactory, for by the time the flowers reach their destination they have lost nearly all their odor. Ten to thirteen hours from the time of picking until the market is reached is practically the limit so far as relates to holding the sweetness of the flower. It is unwise, therefore, to pick the afternoon of one day, and after holding the flowers over night, ship the following morning. It is best, whenever possible, to have the flowers picked early in the morning and reach market the same morning or not later than the middle of the same afternoon. If picked late in the afternoon they should be shipped that night so as to be in the market early the next morning.

The best times for picking are early in the morning and late in the afternoon, that is, between six and eight o'clock in the morning and four and six o'clock in the afternoon. Different plans are adopted in picking and bunching. As a rule, fifty flowers are put in a bunch and the bunch is then backed up with from twenty to twenty-five leaves and tied with violet-colored cord. It is customary in most establishments to do this work directly in the beds. One or two men pick and tie the flowers temporarily in bunches of fifty. Another—more expert in shaping the bunches—unfastens the temporary tie and after arranging the flowers in symmetrical and compact form, picks and adds the leaves and the bunch is then tied permanently. After tying, the bunches are placed in pans of water six inches deep, with cross-bars of laths or other strips to hold the flowers and leaves out of the water. Placed in water in this way the flowers soon stiffen up, and, if kept cool, they lose little of their odor.

Another method, and one we prefer to follow, is to pick the flowers and tie them roughly in bunches of one hundred. They are then carried immediately to a cool bunching room and placed in water. When all is ready they can be bunched by experienced hands and rapidly sorted at the same time. Working in this way two men can pick and bunch from a thousand to twelve hundred an hour. This does not mean merely throwing the flowers together and tying them with a string, but it involves the exercise of taste and judgment in having a symmetrical, yet compact bunch tastefully surrounded by leaves arranged so as to present a neat margin of green. The question of

150   HANDLING AND MARKETING THE CROP.

43.—Picking violets.

bunching is an important one—so important in fact that it often makes a big difference in the price obtained for the flowers. A little time spent in any of our wholesale markets shows this fact strikingly. Good flowers will come in poorly bunched and with a few little straggling yellow leaves sticking out from the center. Such flowers, although good in themselves, are apt to bring fifty per cent less than those from another source tastefully and attractively put up and properly packed. Once in a while, too, in careless bunching a faded or dirty flower is put in. This invariably spoils the bunch and is very apt to knock off profits on the whole shipment. It would pay many growers who complain of poor prices to make weekly visits to their markets, and if they are at all alert they will soon learn that the trouble is not all with the much-abused commission man. So important is the matter of bunching that the grower himself ought to personally attend to it, or at least see that every bunch receives his rigid inspection before it goes out of his hands.

It is customary in shipping to pack either in return or gift boxes. Here also great care must be exercised to make the packages attractive, both on the outside and inside. The more common practice is to use return wooden boxes with hinged lids, each box holding from a thousand to one thousand five hundred flowers. The bunches

44.—Leaves of California violet wired together for bunching flowers.

as they are taken from the water have the stems wrapped in soft tissue paper. The stems are then dipped in water again and the bunches packed closely in the box, stems down. When properly packed the flowers should not shake or mash. Finally the boxes are sealed and are labeled with the grower's name and address.

Before beginning the packing, the boxes are lined with newspapers, with oiled paper next to the flowers. In winter great care has to be exercised to keep the flowers from freezing. It is often necessary to line the boxes with six or seven thicknesses of newspaper in order to keep out frost. In some cases felt is used, but newspapers, being always at hand, are more convenient, and besides are just as serviceable, and in some respects more desirable.

In some cases a plan of packing flowers in wooden boxes provided with trays is followed. Such trays are made about two inches deep and have wire netting on the bottom. The mesh of the netting must be of sufficient size to allow the stems to project through. These make excellent shipping boxes, and by arranging two trays in a box, from one thousand to twelve hundred flowers can be shipped in one package. The same precautions to prevent frost injuries must, of course, be exercised in this case. At this point it is well to emphasize the fact that no matter by what railroad the flowers are shipped, extra precautions must be taken to keep out frost. Although the packages may start out in a well-heated car it is always difficult to foresee what will happen to them before they reach their destination. It is, therefore, necessary to keep a close watch on weather conditions and make the packing in accordance with what the best judgment is in regard to the likelihood of a cold snap.

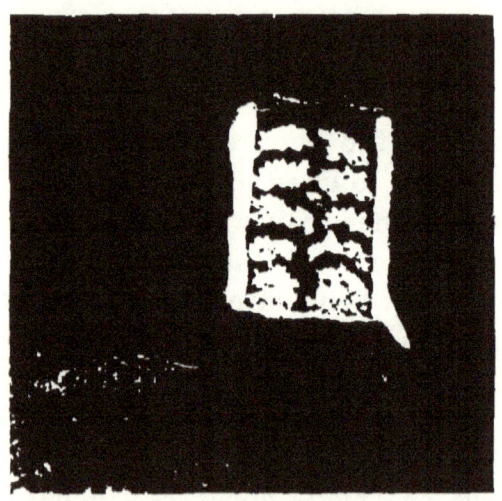

45.—Leatherette shipping box open.

Another very satisfactory means of packing flowers has been recently devised by Mr. P. H. Dorsett. Instead of the wooden boxes, he uses ordinary leatherette telescopes, which he has made to order. These are eighteen inches long, ten inches wide, and seven inches deep. The cover fits over the inside box, and the whole is fastened by a strap at each end. A handle is put on the top so that the package is very easily looked after by the expressmen and others who have to handle it. A wire frame is made to fit inside the box, the meshes of the wire being about half an inch square. Ten holes are cut in the wire, each two inches square, to take the bunches of violets. The frame is made seventeen inches long, nine inches wide, and four inches deep. The stems of the bunches are inserted into the holes and the five

46.—Shipping box showing wire screen for holding bunches.

hundred flowers packed neatly into the box. These packages save considerable expense in express charges. They are, of course, returned, and with good usage, will probably last for several seasons. The cost of these telescopes complete, including wire, is about two dollars each.

In cold weather a second covering, which slips over the entire box, is used. In addition to this quilts made of cotton batting are used, so that there is about an inch of frost-proof material protecting the flowers. As in other cases, the stems of the violets are wrapped in moist tissue paper, and a layer of oil paper, which is put into the box before the flowers are inserted, keeps in the moisture and odor. It has been found by ex-

47.—*Shipping box closed and strapped.*

perience that such packages are handled more gently by express men, and the flowers in all cases reach their destination in excellent shape. Once in a while some are lost through frost, but this seldom occurs, except through the carelessness of the railroad people.

The gift boxes, which are not returned to the

grower, are usually made of three-eighth inch pine. They are deep enough for the bunches in an upright position and hold from eight hundred to one thousand flowers. After being packed and carefully nailed they are wrapped with newspapers or other coverings to exclude the frost. These boxes have some advantages, but they also have many disadvantages, chief of which may be mentioned the fact that the violets in them never make as good a showing as where they are in neat packages, such as already described.

Where the market can be easily reached it is, of course, not necessary to exercise the precautions above mentioned in getting the flowers to their destination. In many cases it is practicable for the grower to take his stock to market in a wagon or to send or take it by train. This is especially the case when dealing with the retailer, and in such instances it is necessary only to see that the flowers are kept from frost and from being unnecessarily shaken or jarred. It is always best, however, to wrap the stems in moist paper, as it has been found by experience that by doing this the flowers are kept fresh and sweet much longer than they otherwise could be. We cannot emphasize too strongly the importance of studying the markets. You must know what is wanted and keep fully posted upon every detail in order to command the best prices.

One feature of marketing violets may be cited here as a suggestion. It is given as a suggestion for the reason that so far as we know it has never been attempted in practice. There seems to be no reason why it would not be profitable to start what could be called a violet store in almost every city of fifty thousand or more inhabitants. In such cases it might not be necessary to use an entire storeroom for the purpose. Some of the large business houses might furnish the desired space, or else room could be procured in other ways. It would, of course, be important to be located in a good business section, the idea being to devote the entire work to the sale of violets, retail and wholesale. By exercising the proper taste in fitting up such a place, taking advantage of all new ideas in the matter of decorations, boxes, ribbons, etc., there seems to be no reason why such an establishment would not prove profitable. It should be the aim of the proprietor of such a place, of course, to not only pander to the wants of customers, but to build up and make fads himself.

Throughout the entire work every precaution must be taken to keep the flowers away from all foreign odors. A new pine box, for instance, may cause trouble. Any objectionable odor, in fact, either in the box, the paper, or the room where the work is carried on, is apt to be taken up by the flowers and to destroy their sweetness.

CHAPTER VIII.

DISEASES AND INSECT ENEMIES.

No hard and fast lines can be drawn between diseases proper and insect attacks. Strictly speaking, a disease is any derangement of the functions of the plant, be it caused by fungous attacks, insect injuries, environment, or a combination of all. For convenience we may discuss the subject under two heads, (1) diseases and their treatment, (2) insect enemies and methods of combating them.

DISEASES AND THEIR TREATMENT.

Probably no other subject connected with violet growing has been so much discussed as the diseases. This is nothing more than might be expected, for the final effects of all proper or improper methods of cultivation are manifested either in the form of health or disease. The plant, in other words, is largely what the grower makes it, and if he thoroughly understood his work there would be little need for writing this chapter. This is equivalent to saying that the question is largely one of knowing how to make the conditions or environment so nearly perfect as to preclude the possibility of disease. It must be understood, of course, that we are dealing with plants in a different way from what they are as we find them in the open air, where they are dependent on water, air, heat, and light as furnished by nature. Under glass man can not only do much toward getting just the plant he wants for the conditions he has, but can approach the problem from another direction and provide the conditions best for his plant. Let us make this point perfectly plain, for few growers appreciate it or realize the real power behind it. Theoretically it will be understood that if the needs of the plant and the environment were exactly balanced, perfect growth would result. Going further, it will be seen that if just the right conditions could be furnished at all times, and the plant through its adaptability were able to meet them exactly, growth would not only be perfect, but life itself would be continuous. We cannot, of course, reach this ideal, but we can strive to approximate it, and this is the gist of all that we have said in previous chapters on soil, watering, feeding, propagation, selection, etc.; so that when it really comes to discussing the diseases there is little additional to say, except to describe the way the plant behaves when diseased and to point out the best line of action in order to once again restore the equilibrium existing between the plant on the one hand and environment on the other.

The really important diseases of the violet are comparatively few in number, and in the order of the injuries they produce may be given as follows: (1) spot, or spot disease; (2) wilt, or stem rot; (3) nanism, or stuntedness; (4) scald, or edge burn; (5) oedema, or wart disease; (6) crown rot, and (7) root galls, or nematodes.

Spot, or Spot Disease. This is generally referred to as "the violet disease," and is recognized by growers generally as the most serious enemy with which they have to deal. Much has been written about it and many theories have been advanced as to its cause. There is no question that spot can be produced in many ways, and may result from the attacks of a number of different fungi. The true spot disease, however (the one which under certain conditions may sweep away an entire field or house of plants in a few weeks), has always associated with it a specific fungus. The fungus is found wherever there is true spot and the spot occurs in this country wherever the violet is grown. There can be no doubt as to the relation of this fungus to the disease, for time and time again the connection has been proved by careful scientific experiments. The fungus itself is an undescribed species of Alternaria, and can be grown, watched, and handled as readily as the violet plant upon which it lives. The writer has never seen a house, a frame, or a field where this fungus was not present, and plants have been examined from Massachusetts to California. Often spotted leaves are found on which even the microscope fails to reveal the presence of the fungus externally. If these leaves are placed in moist air for twenty-four hours, however, an abundant crop of reproductive bodies will be found on the diseased areas.

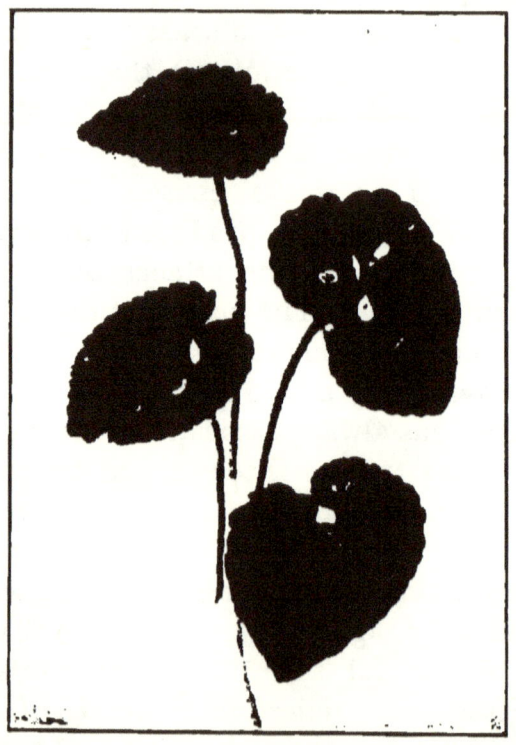

48.—*Spot disease. Early effects on foliage.*

The effects of spot are so well known as to require but little description to recognize them. The first effects, however, are usually overlooked and it is really after the plant has in a measure succeeded in protecting itself that the attention of the grower is called to the injuries. Ordinarily the first indication of a serious attack in a house or in a field is a peculiar odor wholly indescribable, but which once experienced will never be forgotten. It is sickening, and can be approximated by putting a lot of violet leaves in water, placing them in a warm room, and allowing them to wilt.

An examination of the leaves when this odor is first noticed will reveal numerous greenish water-soaked spots, varying in size from a pin head to the blunt end of a lead pencil. There may be only one or two such spots on a leaf; then again the whole leaf and plant may be peppered. This is spot, and two or three badly affected plants in a house will make themselves known to the trained nostrils. Early in the morning, before the ventilators are raised, is the time to catch the odor, or else at night, after everything has quieted down. As the spots enlarge the central portion retains at first a pale greenish yellow color, soon becoming a pale buff, with a more or less distinct margin of umber. Surrounding this is a ring retaining some of the pale yellow green, but almost transparent. Immediately around this is a ring of a green slightly paler than the surrounding portion of the leaf, but appearing darker when held between the observer and the light.

Usually when the spots have reached this stage the semi-transparent ring either becomes trans-

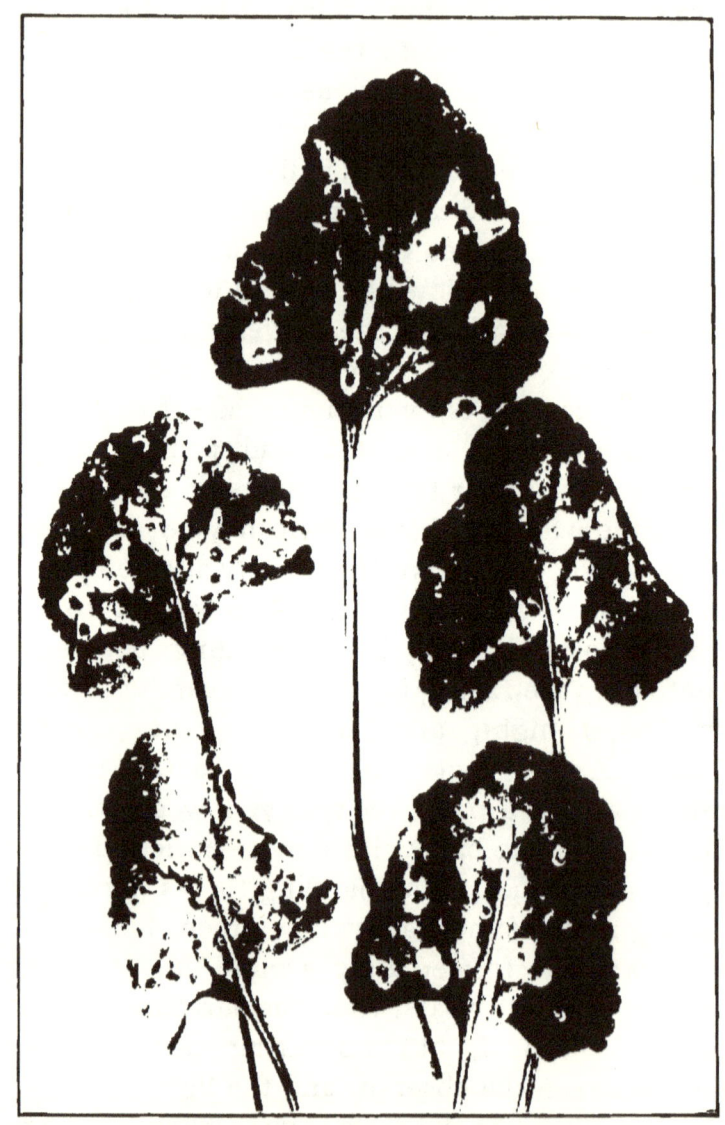

49.—*Spot disease on hardy English Violets.*

parent, in which case the marginal ring almost disappears, or else loses all its green, remaining a pale buff and retaining its marginal ring. Often several adjacent spots unite and form larger ones, but the centers of the uniting spots always remain distinct. Spots which have become entirely transparent except at the center may be included in the enlarging spots, remaining visible as transparent areas in the large buff spot. From the appearance of the small, sunken areas in the center of the spots, many erroneous views as to the relation of insects to the disease have arisen.

A few days of damp, cloudy weather will cause the development of reproductive bodies upon many of the spots. These appear to the naked eye as innumerable blackish, tiny, hair-like points. Each spot is capable of producing thousands of the spores, and each spore is able, under the proper conditions, to germinate and grow, and in so doing infect a healthy leaf or a healthy portion of the same leaf. The spores, as a matter of fact, are wafted about in the air and are constantly settling down on the plants, where they only await favorable conditions to grow into the leaf and produce other spots. We have made experiments which show that in ten hours of one night, under ordinary conditions existing in a greenhouse, fifty to sixty of these spores will settle on a space three inches in diameter. Every spore is able to produce a spot, and the only reason that they do not do so is probably because the conditions are unfavorable for development.

It is evident from what has been said that the more spotted leaves there are in a house the more chances there are for infection. Here, there-

50.—*Spot disease artificially produced.*

fore, is one of the most important points in keeping the disease in check: Every spot must be removed and burned as soon as it is seen, and in no case must the diseased leaves be thrown into the walk or behind the pipes to rot and spread the fungus. When a leaf is badly affected it is best to remove it entirely, but when there are only a few spots on a leaf, these can be pinched or cut out and the rest of the leaf saved.

It is folly to postpone this work, for every day adds to the chances against getting the disease under control. We do not advocate the application of any fungicide. We have tried many things, including Bordeaux mixture, lime, sulphur, ammoniacal solution of copper carbonate, etc., but have never yet found any good evidence that they are beneficial.

In addition to the strictest attention in keeping the plants clean, no effort should be spared to furnish the best conditions for growth. Attend rigidly to watering, ventilating, and firing. Keep all water from the foliage, for wherever the leaves stay wet for seventeen to twenty hours successively spot is pretty sure to develop. From the twentieth of August until the twentieth of November is the period in which spot is most to be feared and watched. If the plants can be successfully brought through this period they are practically safe, unless unusual conditions arise.

From what has been said it will be seen how important it is to have the plants where they will at all times be under control. In frames and in fields this is practically impossible, as there they are constantly exposed to rain and dew. Much benefit may be derived, however, by shading the plants in some way. Rain does not seem to give as much trouble as dew. This is probably owing to the fact that rain washes the spores from the leaves before they have an opportunity to germinate, while in the case of dew the moisture comes on so gradually that the very best conditions are furnished for the germination and development of the fungus. A shading of laths or a screen of any kind will often be sufficient to protect the plants from dew, and thus in a measure ward off the spot. However, it is of the highest importance that the plants be under cover as soon after the middle of August as possible, for wherever they are left outside the danger from infection is very much increased.

Everything that has a tendency to weaken the foliage must be avoided. Too much fertilizer will often cause a tender growth of leaves, and when in such condition spot is very apt to appear if several days of warm, cloudy weather come on. One of the greatest sources of injury is tobacco in the form of smoke. Many growers use tobacco for combating insects, but in our experience it is found very dangerous and apt to cause serious trouble. The nicotine in the tobacco has the power of weakening the tissues to such an extent that the spot fungus finds it an easy matter to infect the foliage. A light fumigation seldom produces any injury, but where several fumigations are made in close succession damage is almost sure to result. Spraying the leaves with tobacco water is apt to produce similar effects, and for this reason we have abandoned the use of tobacco entirely.

Much evidence could be adduced to show the deleterious action of tobacco, but it is not necessary to go into details upon this matter, as one or two examples will suffice. In one instance green aphis was causing considerable trouble in our houses, and in order to destroy it we fumigated heavily with tobacco for two or three nights. Immediately following the fumigation, spot appeared to an alarming extent, and it required several months of hard work and extra precautions to get rid of it. We did not realize at the time the connection of the fumigation with the trouble, but afterwards it was brought to our attention in a number of other ways, and has been proved many times since.

Finally, it may be said that if careful attention has been given to cultural work throughout the entire season, little trouble need be apprehended from this disease. It is only where the grower has been careless in certain directions that trouble is likely to ensue. Many have the unfortunate habit of neglecting little details here and there, and then when the disease appears making a gigantic effort to get rid of it. If attention had been given to minor matters throughout the entire season the chances are that the disease would not have appeared and that there would have been no serious loss in consequence. When the disease has reached a severe form, the flowers are practically worthless and the only thing that can be done is to put forth every effort to get the plants into a healthy condition as soon as possible. Briefly therefore: Keep the plants at all times in a healthy growing condition. Rigidly destroy all diseased parts of the plant. Never apply water to the leaves in such a way that they cannot dry in from four to five hours. Keep the leaves free from dew. Avoid fumigation with tobacco, but if tobacco is used, make the smoke as light as possible.

Wilt, or Stem Rot. Next in importance to spot is wilt, or stem rot. In fact in many sections the stem rot causes more trouble than the spot. The disease is as a rule confined to the stems, although it frequently attacks the roots, but it never produces the injury there that it does when the stems are affected. We have rarely seen a plant wholly free from this trouble, although in many instances it does not produce any appreciable injury. This disease is also due to a fungus, which lives in the tissues and about which comparatively little is known. So far, we know it chiefly through

WILT, OR STEM ROT. 171

its effects, and there can be no doubt as to the relation of the particular species to the disease in

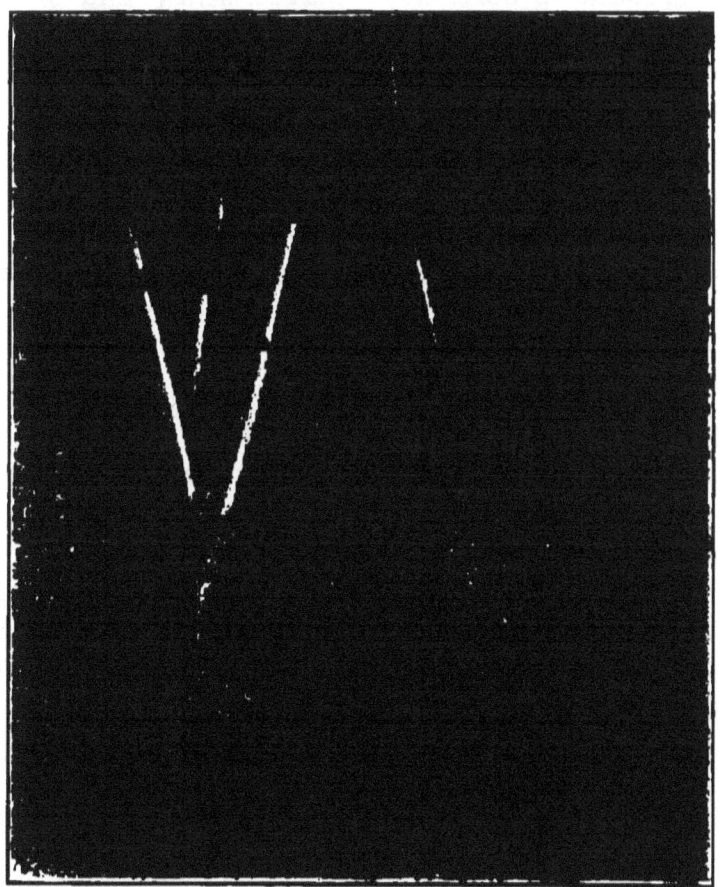

51—*Rooted Campbell cuttings, showing effects of Thielavia on the roots. Plant on left diseased, plant on right healthy.*

question. The fungus is known as Thielavia basicola Zopf, and it attacks other plants besides the violet. It undoubtedly is able to live at certain times on decaying organic matter; in fact, it is found in portions of leaves, straw, and other materials occuring in the sand and soil. From the fact that it occurs on bits of decaying leaves it is important to have the propagating sand absolutely free from organic matter. Infection in a great many cases takes place in the propagating bed and soil. The cutting may root readily and to the casual observer may appear sound, but it is infected nevertheless and later on will show the trouble.

Plants affected with this disease may make a good growth throughout the summer and show no evidence of trouble until September or perhaps October, when they will wilt more or less during the warmer portions of the day and revive during the night. This may go on for a week or more, but finally they wilt completely and die. An examination of such plants shows that the main stem has been practically girdled by the fungus, and that both the water and the food supply have thereby been effectually cut off. The alternate wilting and reviving of the plants is due to the fact that the fungus does its work slowly and thus it requires considerable time to completely encircle the stem. The fact of the matter is, a plant of this kind is probably infected early in its life and for months the fungus slowly grows, gradually destroying cell after cell until finally the plant collapses.

Unquestionably another fruitful source of infection comes about through the practice of pulling off partly decayed leaves from the young plants as they are growing. It is, of course, necessary to keep the plants clean, but in all cases a knife should be used for trimming both leaves and cuttings. If a leaf is pulled off it frequently leaves a scar on the stem and this scar offers an excellent opening for the fungus, which is likely to be present in the soil or on decaying bits of organic matter surrounding the plant. If the leaf is cut off, leaving a short stem, the wound heals before the fungus has an opportunity to gain entrance.

The method of propagation has an important bearing on the trouble and for this reason we have been profuse in our statements regarding the importance of using only vigorous stock. The practice of dividing the plants carries some of the disease over each year, and it will be seen that if this is kept up it is only a question of time when the stock will become so weakened as to be practically worthless. The advantage of rooting cuttings in sand that is absolutely clean is also apparent, for in such cases the fungus, which might be in the young roots taken from the soil, is eliminated. Where the plants are simply divided and even where they are removed as offshoots early in the spring, the young roots often show the disease. The difficulty, however, is most serious where the fungus has attacked the stem, for in such cases the plant will eventually succumb. When a rootlet is once affected it may be destroyed and still the working of the plant need not necessarily be seriously interfered with. Continuous use of the same soil is also a fruitful source of propagating the disease. The longer the soil is used, of course, the more decaying roots there will be present and the more chances for infection through such material.

Summarizing, therefore, the principal ways of holding this disease in check are careful attention to the propagation of stock, extreme care as to the kind of sand and soil employed, and the exercise of rigid precautions in the matter of examination of plants before they are finally set in the beds.

Nanism, or Stuntedness. The dwarfing and stunting of a plant is not generally looked upon as a disease. Nevertheless, so far as we are concerned, it is a true disease because it has a marked effect in reducing the income. It is not uncommon to find among a number of violet plants some which show quite different characters from the ordinary, so far as size is concerned. In such cases the whole plant is more or less dwarfed. The leaves are small, the leaf stalks are short, and the offshoots which go to make up the crown are also short. When such a plant blooms the flower stalks are also short and the flowers in most cases are small.

Of course this dwarfing, or stuntedness, varies much in degree. Some plants will not be more than one-fourth the normal size, while there will be all grades between this and where the dwarfing is so slight as to be hardly recognizable.

52.—*Plants stunted by strong fertilizer.*

An examination of such plants reveals the fact that no external agencies in the nature of fungi or insects have caused the trouble. The roots appear to be free from organisms of all kinds, and the stems and leaves are also free, except in some cases, where red spider may be present, but not in sufficient quantity to account for the dwarfed growth of the plants.

This dwarfing or stunting may be brought about by a number of causes. Anything in fact which has a tendency to check growth may result in permanent dwarfing, but it is particularly at the time when the plant is young that injury is likely to occur. It sometimes happens that the cuttings when taken from the parent plant are not fully mature, and if rooted in sand or soil at this time they will never make as strong or vigorous plants as those made from fully ripened wood. Again, the wood may become so hard that its growth is to a certain extent fixed. Such a cutting would also be apt to produce a dwarfed plant, for the reason that the check which it has received can never be entirely overcome. On the other hand, the wood may be of the proper nature and the cutting in all other respects good, and yet in handling after it is separated from the parent plant, certain checks may be brought about which will result in permanent injury and a dwarfed or stunted plant. Too much or too little water in the propagating bed may bring about these results. Lack of water is often a fruitful source of injury in this connection. The plants do not necessarily have to be dried out to such an extent that they wilt, but the gradual withholding of a sufficient amount of water has a tendency to cause all the growing cells to assume a fixed form, and from this they never recover even after they are moved into more favorable conditions. After the plants are rooted, furthermore, injuries of the same kind may occur.

It may happen that in planting, warm weather comes on, and as a result it is difficult to keep the plants supplied with a sufficient amount of moisture and the roots in consequence will be injured. This results finally in a permanent check, from which the plant never fully recovers. Furthermore, if plants are exposed to too much bright sunlight they are apt to become stunted on account of the intensity of both heat and light. This shows the necessity of some kind of shade through the growing season, for the violet naturally does not grow in the open, but as a rule is found in shady, moist places, away from the direct effects of the sun.

From what has been said in regard to the cause of the trouble, the means of preventing it will become apparent. Every effort should be put forth to keep the plant in a thoroughly healthy growing condition from the time it is started until it is thrown out in the spring. No checks of any kind should be allowed, for the more there are of these the more likely is the output of flowers to be reduced. This only emphasizes the statement already made, that diseases are largely the result of improper methods of culture, and the overlooking of important facts in regard to handling the plants.

Scald, or Edge Burn. This disease as a rule is not serious, although under certain conditions it may become quite troublesome and materially affect the yield of flowers. It manifests itself first by the edges of the leaves turning a yellowish

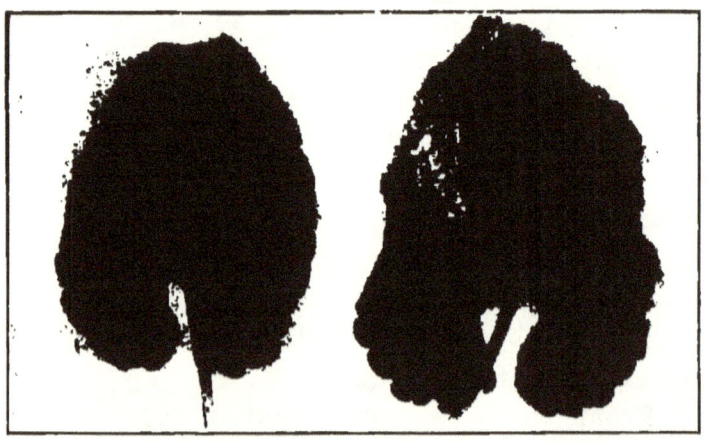

53.—Edge burn, brought on by cold soil.

green. A few days later this color may gradually fade out to almost white, and eventually the entire edge of the leaf will become a papery whitish color. The trouble is usually confined to a rim running around the outer edge of the leaf. This rim varies in width from one-sixteenth to one-quarter of an inch. Under exceptional circumstances nearly the entire leaf may be involved, and there is then left only a small green area in the center. Once the injury is done, there is of course no remedy, and all efforts should be made to keep the plants in such a condition that the trouble cannot be brought on.

One serious after effect of the difficulty is the liability of the plant to be attacked by a number of species of fungi. Although fungi are not the direct cause of the trouble, there are many species which will attack partly dead tissues and from them extend into the healthy parts of the leaf. It is not uncommon, therefore, to find plants affected with this scald, or edge burn, collapsing from the effects of fungi which have first attacked the diseased portions and through them have gained sufficient strength to destroy the unaffected parts of the leaves.

A species of Botrytis is very apt to work on such affected parts, especially if the weather is damp and the sun does not shine for several days in succession. The tissues in such cases get soft and slimy and it is very difficult to keep the plants clean.

The trouble may be brought on by a number of causes. It is often the result of using strong liquid manure, either organic or in the form of chemical fertilizers. Such liquids when applied to the soil and roots seem to temporarily check the

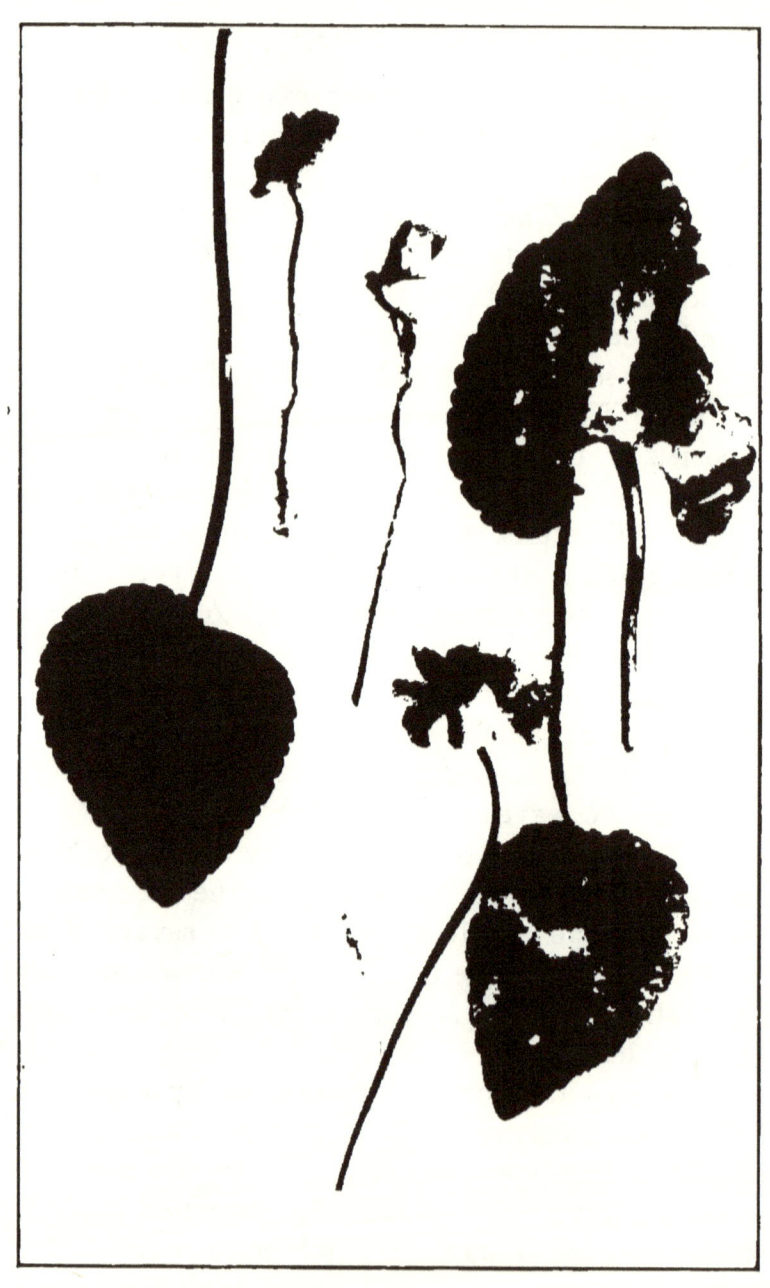

54.—Leaves and flowers injured by Botrytis.

latter to such an extent that they cannot take up water or food. In case the sun is warm at such times and the light bright the young and tender portions of the leaves, namely, the edges, will not have sufficient moisture to serve for growth. If these conditions continue the moisture stored in the cells is used up and then the latter collapse as a result. The disease may be brought on by allowing the soil to get too cold. It is quite common to see plants next to the outer walls of the house showing this difficulty. This is especially the case where there is no air space between the bed proper and the outer wall. The cold from the outside is sufficient to stop the proper working of the roots, and in consequence the parts of the plant above ground suffer as described

In certain types of heavy soils, that is, soils containing too much water, the trouble is likely to occur. It must be understood that the roots of plants require air as well as water. If all or nearly all the air spaces in the soil are filled up with water the roots will suffocate and the plants in consequence suffer. The difficulty resulting from cold soil can easily be overcome for the reason that it is rarely found except around the edges of the house. A board set in so as to intervene between the wall and the soil outside is often sufficient to prevent the trouble. It is better, however, to have two boards, with a space of four or five inches between. This allows an air space and the air in the house is sufficiently warm to keep the soil in the beds next to the board warm enough for root growth.

By attending to the conditions mentioned, looking carefully after watering, and seeing that the soil is not too heavy, little trouble need be feared from this disease.

Oedema, or Wart Disease. This trouble often proves quite serious, but is easily kept under control by the proper handling of the plants. The affected plants show wart-like growths over the leaves and these are usually of a brownish color. These warty growths vary in size, some of them being quite small and others one-eighth of an inch long and one-sixteenth of an inch high. The corky growths are not confined wholly to the leaves. In fact, they frequently occur on the leaf stalks and sometimes on the flower stalks also. It is found that where these warty formations are developed the whole leaf is in a peculiar condition. It is brittle and when taken in the hand cracks very easily. The leaves, in other words, instead of having a live, elastic feel, appear to the touch to be dry like a shaving, and when bent will break with a cracking noise. Wherever a break of this kind occurs the corky growth appears in time. The corky formations may also develop wherever an insect punctures the leaves. The punctures of aphides and the bites

OEDEMA, OR WART DISEASE. 183

of spiders cause many of these swellings. When the plant gets into this condition it is practically unfit for flowering, and when badly diseased it is

55.—*Oedema, or wart disease.*

very difficult to ever get it into proper shape again. The trouble is one that is brought on gradually by improper relations between the moisture of the soil, moisture of the air, and the light.

Where plants are mulched and the soil kept constantly wet the trouble is likely to follow, especially if heavy shading is adopted. Where the plant is grown for some time under these conditions all of its tissues get into a dropsical or oedemic state, and it needs only an injury of some kind to cause the formation of the wart-like growths. If the conditions are very favorable, injuries are not necessary for the wart-like growths, as they will be produced by the plant without intervention of anything of this kind. This is due to the fact that the plant is really making an abnormal effort at growth and the warts are nothing more than excessive growth of the cells at particular points. This trouble seldom occurs in houses properly lighted and ventilated. In underground pits and in outdoor frames where heavy shading is used it is apt to occur, especially if the practice of mulching is adopted.

By paying proper attention to light, ventilation, and watering, little or no difficulty is experienced from the trouble. In case it is seen that plants are becoming oedemic it will be necessary to at once modify the surroundings to such an extent as to admit more light to the leaves and more air to the soil. It will not do, however, to bring about these changes too rapidly. Light should be gradually given and the amount of water added to the soil should be slowly diminished. If the change is too abrupt serious consequences may result, as the plant having been grown under such abnormal conditions is not able to withstand the unusual exposure to bright light and dry soil which the sudden change might bring about.

56.—*Crown rot.*

Crown Rot. This trouble is very apt to occur after the opening of the blooming season, especially if the crowns are heavy and too much water is used for syringing or other purposes. It is often found in houses made of sash, where the drips keep the crowns of the plant constantly wet for days at a time. In such cases the inner or youngest leaves of the crown become softened and through the action of several species of fungi are in a short time reduced to a soft, slimy mass.

The trouble is sometimes quite serious, as all the young inner growth is destroyed and the flower buds of course perish with them. The difficulty, as already pointed out, is brought about largely by the improper use of water. Of course in houses where there are many drips it is impossible to keep the crowns dry. As soon as the trouble is noticed, however, the diseased leaves should be cleaned out as rapidly as possible, the remaining leaves pushed apart, and the crowns opened so as to admit light and air. Where the crowns are very heavy some advantage may result by trimming out part of the leaves, but this of course will more or less interfere with the flowering of the plant.

A mixture of equal parts of air-slacked lime and flowers of sulphur is frequently beneficial in cases of this kind. The two materials should be thoroughly mixed and thrown into the crown with considerable force so as to reach the rotting parts. Lime alone is beneficial, but the sulphur has a tendency to destroy the fungi present and in a measure to check the growth of other organisms. In properly constructed houses, where the drip is reduced to a minimum, little difficulty is ever experienced from this disease. The trouble is, of course, much more apt to be serious where the plants are over-grown, and for this reason the directions given in regard to proper time of planting and the handling of the plants should be closely followed.

Root Galls, or Nematodes. Although this disease is caused by a minute parasitic worm, it is classified with diseases for the reason that it affects the entire plant and could not be properly treated under the heading of insects. Plants badly infested with nematodes are apt to show a dwarfed growth, the leaves being small and the leaf stalks and flower stalks short. This is what might be expected from the fact that these minute parasites attack the roots and through their action on them cut off the food supply. The infested plants upon being removed from the soil show on the rootlets innumerable small nodules, varying in size from a pin-head to a large pea. Although nematodes are considered by some writers as a great menace to violet growing, we have never seen any serious injury produced by them. In fact, our experience leads us to believe that nematodes, instead of being actually injurious, are more apt to be beneficial. We cannot speak of course of the effects of nematodes where the soil has been allowed to become full of them through neglect and other causes. Where the soil has not been properly handled or where it is allowed to remain in use for several years, nematodes are very apt to infest

57.—*Nematodes, or root galls.*

it to such an extent as to become a serious pest. Ordinarily, however, where the soil is changed every year and where new plants are put in each season the nematodes are not sufficiently numerous to really prove serious. It often happens that some of the best flowering plants will show quantities of nematodes on the roots at the close of the season. So far as appearances go, such plants show no indication whatever of disease, and if it were not for the effect of the nematodes it is very probable that vegetative growth would have been so excessive as to have interfered seriously with the formation of flower buds. We look, therefore, on nematodes as in a measure being able to keep the proper balance between root growth and leaf growth. They act partly as root pruners, so to speak, and by their action have a tendency to cause the plants to throw their energy towards flowering rather than towards leaf production. We would not have it inferred from this that we advocate encouraging the attacks of nematodes, but we do not believe it desirable to go to any great expense, such as steaming the soil, for the purpose of holding them in check. If the soil is properly handled and allowed to freeze thoroughly once or twice in the early part of the season, a large number of the nematodes are probably destroyed. However, no matter what action of this kind is followed there will always be some present, but they need not cause any serious uneasiness.

We have experimented with sterilized soil and have been able to grow plants practically free from the worms. Such plants made a most remarkable growth and the leaf development was so great that it seriously interfered with the production of flowers. Furthermore, we found that the plants were making such rapid growth and were becoming so tender and soft at the approach of the spot season that great difficulty was experienced in warding off this disease. On the whole, this question may be summed up by saying that by proper attention to the care of the soil and of the plants little trouble need be apprehended from nematodes, and it will not be necessary to adopt the expensive method of sterilizing the soil.

INSECTS AND OTHER PESTS.

Red Spider. This little pest, which is really not a spider, but a mite, is one of the worst enemies with which violet growers have to deal. It is present at all seasons of the year and is ready at all times to begin its destructive work if allowed to do so. It is difficult to estimate the damage these mites do to plants, for the reason that it is seldom that any plants are entirely free from them and no fair comparisons can therefore be made. Ordinarily when there are only a few of the mites present the plants show no external evidence of their attacks. As the numbers increase, however, the leaves gradually become yellowish and dwarfed, and eventually the whole plant succumbs, unless action is taken to rid it of the pest.

Cuttings or young rooted plants are especially liable to be seriously injured by spider. This is particularly true in spring after the growing season starts. The mites multiply rapidly at this time, and unless the plants are carefully watched they will soon be so badly infested that it will be exceedingly difficult to restore them to a normal condition. In fact, it is questionable if a plant once badly infested with spiders can ever be restored to the normal state. The mites by their action slowly reduce vitality, and not only one, but all functions of the plant are probably more or less affected by them. In this way the whole nature of the plant is more or less changed as it is really suffering from a slow starvation. It will be seen, therefore, that the ultimate effects will be a checking or stunting of some kind, and, as already pointed out, everything of this nature must be carefully avoided.

On plants which have been grown the entire winter in a house or even in frames, the mite sometimes develops to such an extent in late spring as to entirely destroy all growth. Millions of spiders will be found on the foliage, and their webs, which are rarely seen under ordinary conditions, stretch from plant to plant and spiders of all sizes will be found passing rapidly over them and congregating in swarms like bees.

An examination of the leaves of violets infested with spiders, shows mites of various sizes and the eggs from which they are hatched will also be found present in varying numbers. Ordinarily the eggs are spherical and almost colorless. Under a slight magnification they appear like

58.—*Nozzle used in spraying plants for the destruction of red spider.*

little globules of dew, but upon touching them they are found to have relatively firm walls. The eggs are not hatched for eight or ten days after being deposited, the length of time depending in a large measure on warmth and other surroundings. When newly hatched the spiders are very light in color. In fact, it is difficult to distinguish them from the masses of web and the yellowish portions of the affected leaf. As the spiders grow older they molt several times, and finally attain full size, when their color is more or less yellowish red. The color, however, varies greatly and it is seldom that any lot on two different plants are found to be exactly alike.

The mites are exceedingly difficult to kill and for this reason great care must be exercised in not allowing them to attain sufficient numbers to seriously check the growth of the plants before putting forth efforts to destroy them. It is the general belief among florists that spiders do not thrive in moist air, but this does not seem to be the case, for if proper conditions are present moist air alone is not sufficient to hold them in check.

Tobacco, either in the form of smoke or applied in other ways, has little effect upon the mites themselves and probably does not injure the eggs in the least. Fumigation, therefore, is useless in this connection. What is true of tobacco will also hold good with other poisonous gases, such as cyanide gas, which is now coming into general use for greenhouse work. When we first commenced using the cyanide gas we were hopeful that it would prove valuable in destroying spider. It is true that spiders subjected to the fumes of this gas are stupified for a time, but they soon recover and in a few hours are as active as ever.

Soaps of all kinds are effective in destroying both old and young mites, and also kill a large proportion of the eggs. On account of the difficulties in using soap, however, it cannot be generally recommended, but for certain purposes, which will be referred to later, it will be found very useful.

Water applied to the foliage is the only effective remedy that can be depended upon for this pest. It must be applied, however, with considerable force, the object being to wash both mites and eggs from the leaves. To do this successfully and at the same time not injure the plants and not bring about conditions favorable for other diseases, such as spot, is a difficult problem. The chief point in this work is to keep the spiders so thoroughly in check that by the time the plants have attained nearly their full growth in the fall, that is, by the middle of September, spraying can be entirely stopped, and from that time on during the winter little or no water need be applied to the foliage. We have found that where spiders are washed from the leaves a certain per cent of them get back. Many are killed by the direct crushing action of the water, and thousands not destroyed in this way are knocked off into the soil and probably starve to death before they can again reach food. From two to three per cent of all mites on the leaves manage to get back, however, and this shows the importance and necessity of constant attention in the matter of spraying.

If the young plants are perfectly free from spider when set out in the spring it is comparatively easy to keep them so by spraying from two to three times a week for the rest of the growing season. However, if cuttings are rather badly infested with spider we recommend their treatment before planting with a solution of soap. We have tried many soaps but the best results have been obtained from ivory soap, used at the rate of one five cent cake to six or seven gallons of water. The soap should be shaved up with a small plane and dissolved with about one gallon of hot water, and then sufficient cold water added to make the quantity mentioned. By using a small hand spraying pump, which can readily be purchased in the market for four dollars and fifty cents to five dollars, the leaves can be thoroughly wetted with the soap solution at a comparatively slight expense in the matter of material. Five gallons, in fact, will be sufficient to treat three or four thousand cuttings, provided they are in flats and are easily within reach. Allow the soap to remain on the plants two or three hours, then thoroughly syringe with clear water. This treatment should be repeated two or three times, until the spiders and eggs have been destroyed. When used in this way the soap has no deleterious effects on the plants and has a tendency to protect and clean the foliage much better than any preparation we have used. Tobacco water is sometimes used for this purpose, and a tobacco solution made from an extract is also applied. We do not recommend these preparations, however, because they have a tendency to weaken the foliage.

It must be understood that it is not safe to use strong soaps, such as whale oil and soft soaps, because they are very apt to injure the foliage and are not so active in killing the mites as the ivory soap. Spiders treated with ivory soap die in one or two minutes after the solution is applied. When viewed under a microscope full grown spiders show anxiety to get rid of the soap as soon as it reaches them. This lasts only for a few seconds, however, and then the spider quickly folds its legs beneath itself and for a few seconds there may be some violent movements of the legs and other parts of the animal. Even if moved to fresh water a few minutes after soap is applied they seldom revive, which shows how effectually the soap operates.

For cuttings, therefore, the soap solution as recommended will be found exceedingly valuable. We do not consider it advisable to continue the application of soap throughout the entire season, for the reason that we believe it has a tendency to interfere with growth. After the plants are put out, however, spraying with water should be regularly practiced, as before described, and for this purpose it will be found desirable to devise some means of getting on the minimum amount of water with the maximum amount of force. It will require a pressure of at least twenty to twenty-five pounds to prove effective against spider. To get the water on, however, without drenching the beds is often a rather difficult matter, and for this reason we have devised a simple spraying tip, which is found to answer the purpose admirably. This spraying tip may be attached to the end of a three-quarter inch hose, or where the beds are wide we prefer to use a short lance made of light brass pipe. This lance is one-quarter inch in diameter and usually about two feet long. The spraying tip is fastened to one end, while the other end is provided with a connection to screw on to the three-quarter inch hose. The tip itself consists merely of a piece of brass flattened out at the end and provided with a narrow slit, through which the water is forced. This slit is so adjusted that the water issues through it in much the shape of a gas flame, but, of course, very much larger. At a distance of twenty to twenty-five inches from the end of the slit the water breaks up into innumerable fine drops, which are thoroughly effective in washing the spiders from the leaves and not injuring the latter in the least. With a little practice the beds can be gone over quickly with this device, and the under side of the leaves may be so thoroughly washed that the spiders will have little opportunity for development. If this practice is followed throughout the growing season the plants will be able to go into winter quarters practically free from the pest, and will, therefore, require little additional work of this kind during the winter. Whenever it is necessary to spray during the winter, the work must be done on a bright day so that the plants will dry off in a few hours. Never spray later than eleven o'clock, otherwise the crowns will remain wet during the night.

Green and Brown Aphides. Every violet grower is probably familiar with these insects. Up to six or eight years ago the green aphis was about the only one that ever proved troublesome. Whether there is more than one species of green aphis which attacks the violet is not known. They can be found nearly always, and it requires only slight neglect for them to soon become exceedingly troublesome. The green aphis, with which every grower is generally familiar, attacks both leaves and flowers, but it is particularly the latter that are likely to show the most serious effects of the pest. Ordinarily, when the leaves are infested the aphis is first found on leaves which have begun to fade. The yellow leaves harbor the insect, but it soon gains sufficient strength, if neglected, to spread to perfectly healthy leaves and from them to the flowers. In watching plants, for the green aphis, therefore, it is always best to keep a close eye on the yellowish leaves as they are picked off. If the green fly is found upon them immediate steps must be taken to check it before it has increased sufficiently to spread to other parts of the plant.

When the fresh and growing leaves become infested, and when it spreads to the flowers and young buds, the matter becomes serious and heroic efforts will be required to get rid of the pest. It is when the insect turns its attention to the flower buds and flowers that the most serious trouble results. The aphis crawls into the very young buds and through its punctures and the sucking of the juice the flower is very much distorted and is made practically worthless. Two or three of these insects in a bud will so injure it that the flower will be valueless. When they occur in great numbers and the buds and flowers are badly infested the former have a speckled or spotted appearance quite unlike what they should be. Instead of the beautiful mauve color, the petals have whitish blotches scattered over them, and this detracts greatly from their appearance and makes them practically worthless so far as selling is concerned.

Five or six years ago the brown aphis began to attract attention among violet growers. This insect is reddish brown in color and resembles somewhat the one which attacks the chrysanthemum. We first observed the insect three or four years ago on some plants obtained from Massachusetts. Soon after this we saw it in other localities, and now it seems to be pretty generally distributed throughout the violet growing regions of the East. This aphis seems to be a new form—at least no record can be found of anything like it attacking violets in this or other countries. Be this as it may, the effects of the insect are serious. In fact it is a more formidable foe than the green one. Instead of attacking the older and more resistant leaves, the brown aphis as a rule will be found on the most tender growth just as it unfolds from the crown. In consequence of this habit of the insect the plants are severely crippled. The young leaves are attacked as fast as they appear, and the plants in consequence are so thoroughly checked and stunted that little or no growth takes place. It will be found at all seasons of the year, but is particularly active through the growing season, that is, from about the middle of May until the middle of October. It seems to be more troublesome in houses than in the open air or in frames, but this may be accounted for perhaps by the fact that the insect is less liable to the attacks of natural enemies under glass and has a better opportunity, therefore, of propagating itself. Like the green aphis, it also attacks the flowers, but seems to prefer the foliage, and as a rule is confined to it. Both the green and the brown aphis are more or less injured by cold, but still they cannot be entirely killed by freezing, as we have reason to know from experience in growing plants in frames, where the temperature fell as low as six or eight degrees below zero. In such cases many aphides were destroyed, but enough survived to start a new brood as soon as the weather became favorable.

The almost universal remedy against aphides under glass has, up to the past few years, been tobacco. Fumigation has been the principal method followed, the ordinary tobacco stems being used for the purpose. Probably in some sections fumigation with tobacco will continue to be used, as it is undoubtedly the simplest and cheapest method of combating these pests.

We have already pointed out, however, the serious objections to the continued use of tobacco. This is especially the case in certain regions where the use of tobacco is more apt to bring on spot than in other sections. Where it is necessary to use tobacco, great care must be exercised, and the grower should never wait until the insects have accumulated in numbers, otherwise the smoke will have to be made so strong that injury to the plant in one form or another is sure to follow. Light fumigations, given at regular intervals, will probably hold both kinds of aphides in check, but aside from the objections already mentioned there are others of a serious nature which must also be considered where tobacco is used. As everyone knows, the odor is exceptionably disagreeable and undesirable. This is particularly the case in violets, which readily take up many foreign odors and never fully recover from the effects. It is therefore found undesirable to pick violets in a house which has been recently fumigated with tobacco. In fact at least a week should elapse after fumigation before any picking is done. These reasons, together with others which have been given, have prompted us to practically abandon the use of tobacco in every form for aphides and insects of this nature.

A good deal has been written about the use of hydrocyanic acid gas for this work. This has been used for a number of years in fumigating plants in the open air, but it is only recently that it has come into general use for greenhouse purposes. Through the efforts of Messrs. Albert F. Woods and P. H. Dorsett, who have been associated with the writer in work on plants under glass, experiments were inaugurated several years ago to test the value of this gas in the greenhouse. At this time we were having serious difficulty with our violets from the attacks of aphides, and it was a question as to whether it would not be necessary to either give up growing the crop or adopt some method of getting rid of the pest other than those usually followed. After many experiments it was found that the gas could be used with perfect safety for fumigating violets. Moreover, the flowers a few hours after the gas had been used were perfectly sweet and showed no effects whatever from the action of the gas. From time to time various changes were made as to the methods of application, until finally the practice has developed into a comparatively simple operation, which may be described as follows:

In all cases where fumigation with this gas is to be followed it is necessary to first determine accurately the cubic contents of each house. The determination of the cubic contents of the house while in itself a comparatively simple problem, has, in the eyes of many growers, difficulties which they are not willing to undertake. The cubic contents can be determined by a comparatively simple mathematical calculation, but perhaps the easiest way is by a method recently described by the writer in the *Florists' Exchange.** This method involves nothing more difficult than the mere counting of a number of squares, and from an examination of the accompanying illustration the simplicity of the method will become apparent. Procure from a stationery store or art supply store some cross-section paper, such as represented in the figure. In this particular case squares of three sizes are shown, the largest being one-half inch, the next one-fourth inch, and the smallest one-sixteenth inch square. The one-

**Florists' Exchange*, Vol. II, No. 5.

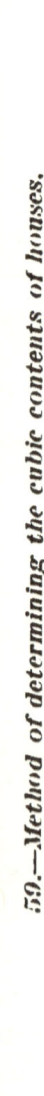

Fig. 59.—Method of determining the cubic contents of houses.

fourth inch squares may represent feet. Now determine the dimensions of the house, that is, the length, width, height to ridge, and height on sides, and make a sketch as shown, each square, or one-fourth inch, representing one square foot. This particular house, it will be seen, is eighteen feet (eighteen squares) wide, twelve feet to the ridge, six and one-half feet high at the back, and four and one-half feet high in front. The ridge stands five feet from the back wall, as shown in the sketch. After the lines are drawn, simply count the squares inclosed, and the number of squares will be the number of square feet. The parts of squares, that is, where a line divides a square, can be easily determined by counting the smallest squares or by the eye, and by adding these fractions of squares together the number of whole squares may be readily found. After the number of square feet is obtained it is only necessary to multiply this by the length of the house in feet and the result will be the cubic contents. For example, supposing the house in question is one hundred feet long, it contains one hundred and fifty and one-half squares, or square feet, and one hundred and fifty and one-half multiplied by one hundred equals 15,050 cubic feet. The whole operation requires less time than it takes to describe it and will apply of course to a house of any shape or size. It may be added that if the cross-section paper cannot be obtained readily the sections or squares can be laid off with a rule and lead pencil and practically the same results obtained. In any event, it is only necessary to get an accurate outline drawing of the section of the house and by projecting this over squares as indicated the number of square feet in the section can be readily determined.

The gas is made by combining potassium cyanide (ninety-eight per cent pure) and commercial sulphuric acid. It has been found by experiment that for violets 0.15 of a gram (one gram equal fifteen and a half grains avoirdupois) of ninety-eight per cent cyanide of potassium will be required for each cubic foot of space in the house, and from these data it is easy to figure out the exact amount of cyanide of potassium wanted for a given amount of greenhouse room. When the cubic contents have been determined and 0.15 of a gram of the cyanide of potassium has been weighed out for each cubic foot, the next step is to crush all the large lumps and place the cyanide in paper bags so as to have it ready for use in the house. We usually use two bags, one within the other, for the purpose, in order to insure perfect safety. For a house one hundred feet long and twelve feet wide there should be provided two ordinary earthenware jars, each holding about two gallons. These jars should be placed in the walk, about equal distances apart and equal distances from each end of the house. As soon as the proper quantities have been put in the bags, the latter are taken to the jars and then a string is arranged so that each jar will have suspended directly over it one of the bags containing the cyanide. The end of the string is then run out to the door and can be easily tied so as to hold the bags in position just above the jars. The string can be easily run through screw eyes fastened to the sash bars or by some other method which will readily suggest itself to the operator. Everything being in readiness pour enough cold water into the jars to about cover the amount of potash in the bags. As soon as the water is poured in bring the acid forward and slowly add this to the water until steam begins to rise. When the steam commences to show stop pouring in the acid and arrange the next jar in the same way. While doing this it is best to have the bags of cyanide rest on the ground. The water and acid now being ready readjust the bags in their proper places so that they will drop directly into the jars when the string holding them is loosened. The operator now goes to the door and by taking hold of the string allows the bags to drop directly into the jars. The door is then closed and in about a minute (sometimes less) the violent action of the chemical changes can be heard. No attempt whatever must be made to enter the houses at this time, for by doing so death would unquestionably result in a few seconds. Previous to setting off the gas all the ventilators must be put down, and if the house is loose it is well to sprinkle the roof with water. Arrangements must be made, however, for opening some of the ventilators from the outside. From the time the gas begins to generate it should be allowed to remain twenty minutes in the house and then the doors and ventilators should be opened from the outside and air freely admitted. When opening the ventilators from the outside take care not to breathe the gas. The house should not be entered under any circumstances for half an hour, for it will take at least that time for the fumes to be driven out.

Unless the aphides are very abundant it will not be necessary to use the gas more than once a month during the growing season. However, the fumigation should not be done at regular periods, but should be carried on whenever there is sufficient evidence that aphides are increasing in undesirable numbers. This treatment never fails to do the work when proper care is taken, and there is no injury whatever to foliage or flowers.

Cut Worms. The leaves of violets are sometimes attacked and injured by cut worms. This is especially the case in late spring after the new plants have been put out. The cut worms, as a rule, are more troublesome in houses where sash are removed or where the sides are open. There appear to be several species of these insects, and as the worms are voracious eaters, they can in a short time do considerable damage to small plants. It is not uncommon to find young plants having only six or eight good leaves, completely cut down by these pests. Sometimes the worms instead of cutting off the leaves will cut off the stems, and of course in such cases the plant is ruined. The worms appear to be the same kind as those which feed upon grasses. In fact where grass is allowed to grow around the houses and in the beds, the insects are, as a rule, much more apt to be troublesome. The worms are often found an inch and a half in length, and it is seldom that they can be seen on the plants in the day time, unless in cloudy weather or in dark places.

About all that can be done in the way of holding this pest in check is to watch the plants carefully, and at the first evidence of injury to search for the worms and detroy them. As a rule, if the worms are not found on the plant, they will be discovered just beneath the surface of the ground near the stem. By digging in the soil around the plants, the insect can be brought from its hiding place and destroyed. In closed houses, where fumigation is practiced, the cut worms are of course destroyed, but in the field and in frames the collection and destruction of the pest, as already stated, is about all that can be recommended. The fact that these worms live upon grasses shows the importance of keeping the beds perfectly clean, and also the importance of keeping the ground perfectly clean of grass for a considerable distance around the frames or the beds if the latter are made in the field. So far as our observations go, the moth, which deposits the eggs from which the cut worms are hatched, seldom if ever selects the violet. The eggs are more likely to be deposited on grasses and other plants, and from these the worms reach the violet. It frequently happens that growers are neglectful about keeping old beds and the corners of houses free from weeds and grass. It is not uncommon to allow grass and weeds to grow up behind the beds in some cases, and it is just such places that harbor worms. Rigid attention should therefore be given to cleanliness, which is as important in this case as in any others mentioned.

Sawfly. The leaves of violets during the growing season, that is, from June to September, are sometimes injured by a small caterpillar-like worm, which has been determined by the Entomologist of the United States Department of Agriculture to be the larva of a species of sawfly. This insect sometimes does considerable damage by cutting the leaves, giving the whole plant a ragged appearance. The larva of the sawfly seems to prefer cool, shady places, and, as a rule, is found near the sides of the house or in the shade of the gutters. Picking and destroying the insects is the only satisfactory means of getting rid of them, except where fumigation with the cyanide gas is practiced. In such cases this insect, together with many other kinds, will be effectually destroyed. It sometimes happens that the eggs from which the sawfly larva are hatched are deposited on the young plants while they are still in flats or before they have been transplanted to permanent beds. It will often be found advantageous in such cases to apply some material that will destroy the eggs and young larvæ before the plants are set where they are to stand. For this purpose there is nothing better than the ivory soap solution, the same as recommended for red spider. It can be applied with a hand spraying pump, or the solution can be made up and kept in an ordinary water pail, and the plants as taken up can have their stems and leaves dipped. This, however, is not as satisfactory as spraying, and is resorted to usually only where cuttings are lifted directly from sand and there is no soil adhering.

Gall Fly Maggots. We have never had any difficulty with this pest, but in some sections of the country it has occasioned serious damage. The maggot is very small and is yellowish white in color. It is found, as a rule, in the youngest leaves as they push out from the crown of the plant. The affected leaves as they come out are

60.—Injuries to Violet leaves by gall fly maggots.

badly curled and the maggots are found only where the leaf is curled. The maggots are so abundant that all the leaves become curled in this way, and as a result the whole plant is seriously stunted.

The effects of the maggots are to seriously dwarf the growth of the plants and to practically stop the development of the flower buds. In many cases where the affected leaves are pulled off, the side crowns will start, but they soon become infested with the maggot. The maggot is the larva of a small gall fly, which looks like a miniature wasp. It is not uncommon to find maggots in the soil, and from the latter they seem to be able to reach the young leaves in some way. Whether they pass from the leaves to the soil and there attain the adult state we are not able to say, and so far as we know, this point has not been determined. Our observations lead us to believe that the pest is much more apt to occur in localities where proper attention has not been paid to mixing the soil and to drainage On low, heavy, wet ground the pest is much more apt to be injurious than where good soil is at hand and where drainage is perfect. Certain kinds of manures seem to favor the development of the maggot. Whether it is capable of living in the manure, or on plants alone has not been determined, so far as we are aware. It seems to be a fact, however, that where manure is not clean, that is, where it is mixed with refuse in the shape of garbage and other material, the pest is apt to breed.

There is no satisfactory remedy for this maggot when once it has infested a house. We cannot speak as to the effect of cyanide gas upon it, for, so far as we know, this remedy has not been tried. It is not practicable to pick the leaves, because in such cases the crowns are permanently injured and the flowering is, therefore, either entirely

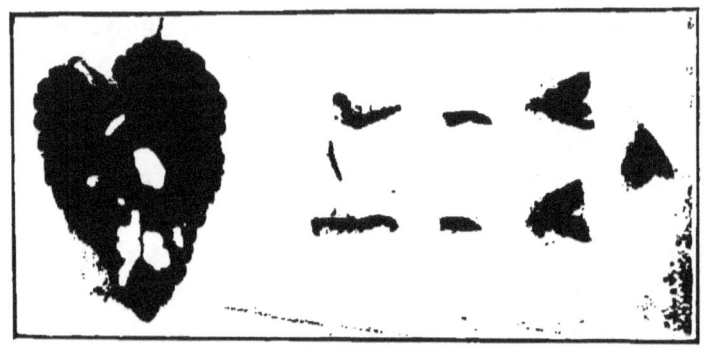

61.—*Larvæ and moths of Phlyctænia ferrugalis.*

stopped or checked. Air-slacked lime thrown into the crowns will be found beneficial. It should be thrown into the plant with considerable force and plenty should be allowed to reach the soil. Following this practice and giving the best cultural conditions possible, such as allowing plenty of air and stirring the soil, is about all that can be suggested in the line of treatment.

Phlyctaenia ferrugalis. Violet plants are

sometimes attacked during midsummer by the larva of a small moth. The insect has been identified for us by the Entomologist of the United States Department of Agriculture under the above name. The larvæ attack the leaves, destroying the softer parts and leaving only the skeleton or framework of the tissues. The illustration does not show this plainly, as the camera does not distinguish the colors sufficiently. Plants grown in shady places are usually most liable to attack. Generally the worms are surrounded by a light web, and occasionally two leaves are fastened together in order to give them protection. The insect never produces serious injury, but is is well to watch for it and take such steps to destroy it as may be practicable. It may be destroyed by picking the leaves containing the larvæ, but by far the best method is fumigation with cyanide gas. Where this gas is used for other pests the insect in question is easily kept in check.

CHAPTER IX.

COST OF PRODUCTION AND PROFITS.

In a matter of this kind it is difficult to give anything but approximate figures. Location, proximity to market, ability to get fuel, soil, and manure, the cost of labor, etc., are all factors that play an important part in making an estimate as to the actual cost of producing the crop. In making an estimate it will be necessary to take into consideration the value of the ground, the cost of houses, and in fact everything connected with the work, just as a commercial man would consider all phases of his business in any effort at determining profit and loss. It will be best to make the estimates on a definite number of plants, as it is easier to figure from this standpoint, as a matter of fact, that the cost of production will be relatively less for ten thousand plants than it is for five thousand. The same will hold true as we decrease the number of plants—that is, five thousand can be grown at relatively less cost than one thousand. There are a number of reasons for this, chief of which is the fact that the more plants there are the more possible it is for the grower to so arrange all of his operations as not to have a loss of material or time. For instance, it costs less relatively to heat houses holding ten thousand plants than it does to neat houses holding five thousand. The same will hold true for labor, for soil, for fertilizers, and in fact for all matters connected with the work.

Under ordinary conditions, such as we find in the vicinity of many of our large cities, we may place the cost of ground and houses sufficient for ten thousand plants at three thousand dollars. In some respects this is an over-estimate, but it is based on the fact that ground used for this purpose is worth not less than five to seven hundred dollars an acre and that the houses are of the same kind as those we have already described. We have therefore to estimate as one of the items of the cost of production the interest on the money invested in houses, ground, and other fixtures connected with the work. We may put this as a total at three thousand five hundred dollars, so that the interest at six per cent would be two hundred and ten dollars. There is also to be considered the question of wear and tear on the houses and other materials used in connection with growing the plants. This may be placed at not less than eight per cent a year. In other words, renovating walks, replacing broken glass, painting, and other necessary repairs will cost not less than two hundred and eighty dollars a year.

The cost of fuel will of course vary widely, but under ordinary conditions, that is, in regions where the temperature seldom goes lower than twelve degrees below zero for any length of time, the amount of fuel necessary to heat houses holding ten thousand plants will probably not exceed one hundred and twenty-five dollars.

The cost of labor, not including that of the grower himself, which is not estimated here, should not exceed three hundred and fifty dollars per year. In other words the grower himself with the assistance of one good man can easily handle ten thousand plants. It may be necessary to make some allowance for the busy season, when possibly an extra man would have to be taken on for a month. With the grower understanding his business it is not necessary to have an expert as an assistant. An ordinary laborer, provided he is quick, active, and willing to work, will answer every purpose. Such help can be obtained for twenty-five to thirty dollars per month. Labor, therefore, we estimate at three hundred and fifty dollars per year. For incidentals, including express charges and various minor matters, we estimate one hundred dollars. These figures will vary, of course, in different localities but are, we believe, a fair average.

Summarized, the total outlay for ten thousand plants per year is as follows :

Interest on money invested in ground, houses, etc......$210
Repairs 280
Fuel 125
Labor 350
Incidentals 100

Total, ... $1,065

The total output of money per year, therefore, in growing ten thousand plants is estimated at one thousand and sixty-five dollars. This is an expenditure of practically ten cents per plant, so that the actual cost of maintaining and growing each plant, basing the estimate on ten thousand plants, is practically ten cents. We have given what in our judgment is a fair average, but of course these figures can be reduced by rigid attention to details and a thorough knowledge of all the points necessarily connected with the work. If the owner is willing to take a hand and to attend largely to the firing and look after the watering and ventilation, the cost will be materially decreased. If, on the other hand, he delegates this work to others he must necessarily pay for it, and in consequence the cost of production will be increased.

Turning our attention now to the other phase of the question, namely, the profits, we are confronted at the outset with the same difficulties as mentioned in the first instance—that is, the profits will depend in large measure on the market, on the ability of the man to properly handle his crop, and above all on the quality of the product.

It must be understood that at first the grower will have to be content with relatively low prices, for the reason that he has yet to make a reputation, and until this is accomplished he may not hope to command from the market the highest returns. There is always an opening for good stock, but, as we have pointed out elsewhere, it is not only necessary to have the stock good, but it is of the highest importance that it should be so handled and so put on the market as to create a demand for it. As soon as the demand is created it is not so difficult to increase prices.

As to the yield of flowers per plant, this will depend altogether on the knowledge of the grower. Ordinarily fifty flowers per plant is considered a good average, but there is no reason why this average should not be increased to seventy-five or even one hundred. The grower should not be content with less than one hundred salable flowers per plant, and his aim and effort should be to succeed in making every plant average this number. On the basis of fifty flowers per plant, however, the total yield from ten thousand plants would be five hundred thousand flowers. If the yield be increased to one hundred flowers per plant the total number of flowers is of course doubled. Now this doubling of the total number of flowers does not mean the doubling of the cost of production at all. In fact the cost of producing one hundred flowers per plant is relatively little more than producing fifty. The main additional item of cost to be considered is that connected with the handling of the crop, which is a relatively small amount. Let us assume, however, that the grower averages fifty flowers per plant, and that he is so situated that the best prices he is able to command will not average over sixty cents per hundred for the season. This will mean that he receives approximately the following prices:

>October flowers............................$0.50 per hundred
>November flowers......................... 0.50 per hundred
>December flowers.......................... 1.00 per hundred
>January flowers............................ 0.75 per hundred
>February flowers........................... 0.50 per hundred
>March flowers............................... 0.50 per hundred
>April flowers................................. 0.50 per hundred
>   Average................................. 0.60 per hundred

The seven months, as already indicated, will give him an average of sixty cents, providing his plants yield as they ordinarily do—that is, a heavy flowering in November, March, and April, with lighter crops during the other months. If he can by a proper handling of his plants and by proper selection so change the flowering period as to get the heaviest yields during the months of December, January, and February, he can, as will readily be seen, increase his average, because the flowers will be worth more at this time. In other words, it is far better to get fifty thousand flowers in December and twenty-five thousand in March than to get twenty-five thousand in December and fifty thousand in March.

It is entirely within the range of possibility to so grow the crop as to materially increase the number of flowers during the regular winter months. The average of sixty cents is comparatively low and should not be considered as the limit by any means. With a reputation established for growing good flowers, and for putting them in the market in a fresh state and always in excellent condition, the range of prices can be materially increased. A good grower should not be content unless he can average the following:

October flowers	$0.50 per hundred
November flowers	0.75 per hundred
December flowers	1.50 per hundred
January flowers	2.00 per hundred
February flowers	0.75 per hundred
March flowers	0.50 per hundred
April flowers	0.50 per hundred
Average	0.90 per hundred

This gives an average for the seven months of practically ninety cents, or an advance over the first figures of thirty cents per hundred. It is figures of this kind that show the possibilities within the reach of the intelligent grower. There is no reason why his flowers should not average him 90 cents, and furthermore there is no reason why each plant should not be grown so as to yield an average of one hundred flowers per plant.

As an example of what may be accomplished we give the yields for eight months of fourteen hundred Lady Hume Campbell plants in one of our houses and the prices, as follows:

October,	1897,	8,000 flowers	$0.50 per hundred
November,	1897,	11,950 flowers	0.75 per hundred
December,	1897,	12,000 flowers	1.00 per hundred
January,	1898,	11,830 flowers	1.25 per hundred
February,	1898,	17,250 flowers	0.75 per hundred
March,	1898,	23,900 flowers	0.75 per hundred
April,	1898,	23,850 flowers	0.50 per hundred
May,	1898,	3,800 flowers	0.50 per hundred
Total		112,580	Average $0.75 per hundred

It will be seen that this house, containing fourteen hundred plants, yielded an average of eighty flowers per plant, and the average price received was seventy-five cents per hundred, so that the value of the yield of each plant was sixty cents.

On the basis of an average of sixty cents per hundred, the total value of the yield from ten thousand plants would be three thousand dollars, or thirty cents per plant. We have already seen that the cost of producing such a plant is ten cents, so that the net profit is twenty cents per plant, or two thousand dollars for the establishment. On the other hand, if the average price obtained were ninety cents per hundred flowers, the net profit would be thirty-five cents per plant, or three thousand five hundred dollars for the establishment. Again, if the average yield is increased, as it should be, to seventy-five or one hundred flowers per plant, the profits will be increased approximately sixty-four and one hundred and twenty-eight per cent respectively.

On the whole, it may be said that the income from ten thousand plants grown in houses and handled properly should year in and year out average five thousand six hundred dollars, while the total expenses should not exceed one thousand five hundred dollars. This means an average yield of seventy-five flowers per plant and an average price of seventy-five cents per hundred flowers.

Violets can be grown in frames cheaper than they can in houses. With good care the total cost per plant will not exceed five cents, or ten cents per hundred for the flowers, reckoning that the average yield of the latter is fifty flowers per plant. Such flowers ought to net the grower fifty cents per hundred, leaving a profit over all expenses of forty cents per hundred, or approximately four dollars per sash. Finally, it must be remembered that while these figures are fair averages, and are based on actual experience, they cannot be approximated without strict attention to every detail.

www.ingramcontent.com/pod-product-compliance
Lightning Source LLC
Chambersburg PA
CBHW031828230426
43669CB00009B/1264